"Love Is the Winningest Thing in the World"

...yet, do you ever let any of these "spoiler attitudes" mar your witness for Christ?

- *Hanging Judge*—judging others, thus avoiding your own shortcomings
- *Sunglass Kid*—shading the truth with lies and deception
- *Touchy Tillie*—withdrawing from others when you don't get your way
- *Pistol Pete*—abusing people verbally

These are just a few of the "spoiler attitudes" Dale Galloway reveals in *Love Can Be Repaired*. Discover how love can transform these childish ways of thinking. Once you make the choice to love, spoiler attitudes will become godly attitudes.

Don't be a loser. Let love be your greatest aim! Find out how to be a winner in *Love Can Be Repaired*.

By Dale Galloway

Dare to Discipline Yourself
Confidence Without Conceit
Love Can Be Repaired

Love Can Be Repaired

DALE E. GALLOWAY

Power Books

Fleming H. Revell Company
Old Tappan, New Jersey

Unless otherwise identified, Scripture quotations in this book are taken from the Holy Bible, New International Version. Copyright © 1973, 1978, 1984 International Bible Society. Used by permission of Zondervan Bible Publishers.

Scripture verses marked TLB are taken from *The Living Bible*, copyright © 1971 by Tyndale House Publishers, Wheaton, Ill. Used by permission.

Scripture quotes marked KJV are taken from the King James Version of the Bible.

Scripture quotations identified PHILLIPS are from THE NEW TESTAMENT IN MODERN ENGLISH, Revised Edition—J.B. Phillips, translator. © J. B. Phillips 1958, 1960, 1972. Used by permission of Macmillan Publishing Co., Inc.

Material from *Broken Members, Mended Body* by Kathy Miller. © Copyright 1989, Regal Books, Ventura, CA 93006. Used by permission.

Library of Congress Cataloging-in-Publication Data
Galloway, Dale E.
    Love can be repaired / Dale E. Galloway.
        p.   cm.
    ISBN 0-8007-5339-9
    1. Love—Religious aspects—Christianity.   I. Title.
BV4639.G336 1990
241'.4—dc20   89-28703
                                                              CIP

Copyright © 1990 by Dale E. Galloway
Published by the Fleming H. Revell Company
Old Tappan, New Jersey 07675
Printed in the United States of America

Contents

Contents

Contents

Love Can Be Repaired

1
Make Love Your Number-One Aim

Love is one of the most powerful forces in life. Although most of us would agree with that statement, we rarely realize the extent to which our lives are shaped by our ability to give and receive love—or by our inability. Whether we are speaking of romantic love, parental love, or friendship, we feel the power of love in the relationship.

Early in a romantic relationship, there seems to be nothing that could possibly threaten our love. The teasing and jealousy of our friends, parental approval or disapproval, hard times or good times, all roll off our backs as long as our loved one is by our side. And when we are apart, the pain is so intense it is almost touchable. People tell us we are experiencing puppy love or infatuation, but we know better than that: This is a love that will last forever!

Sometimes we're right. Oh, the giddiness passes with

time, but as we come to see our loved one more clearly, we are still entranced by what we see, and love deepens with each day that passes, each crisis we share drawing us closer.

Sometimes we're wrong, though. One morning we wake up and feel, "I can't take another day of this!" Whether what's bothering us is superficial or extremely serious, we've had it—and we want out!

Fifty percent of all marriages currently end in divorce. So much for puppy love. The people involved in these relationships go from infatuation to reality to divorce court, sometimes at a mind-boggling speed, leaving behind damaged hopes and dreams and often bewildered children. The sad part is, a good percentage of these marriages could be saved, as could troubled parent-child relationships. With a little patience, maturity, and insight, we *can* learn to love again, if we make love our number-one priority.

Confession of a Reformed Workaholic

Sometimes relationships deteriorate from a simple lack of attention. We work so hard at other goals that we ignore love, and the next time we need it, it's gone.

Most of my life I have been a very goal-oriented person, working hard to achieve worthwhile goals. My lifetime goal has been to build a great church for the unchurched thousands, a church that would heal hurts, build dreams, and provide multiple ministries to meet people at the point of need. For as long as I can remember, I have given my time, my energy, my money, my focus, my life to the pursuit of this magnificent dream. God has honored and blessed this dream and given me the ministry of New Hope Community Church, which helps thousands.

I admit that over the years I have sometimes let my life get out of balance and have forgotten that something is even greater than the pursuit of any dream. However, some years ago while I was reading *The Living Bible*, the Lord gave me what I consider a greater goal: keeping my life in balance. Here it is as I found it in 1 Corinthians 14:1: "Let love be your greatest aim." If you are having trouble keeping your priorities straight, let love be your greatest aim. If you have been having trouble in your marriage because you are not taking the time to work on it, let love be your greatest aim. If you are uptight with others instead of relaxed and happy, let love be your greatest aim.

Can you see that when you make love your number-one aim there is no way on earth you can end up a failure? It's true. You may fail in a business deal; you may lose your job; you may end up with some broken relationships, simply because it takes two people to have a relationship; but if you keep on making love your number-one aim, you will never be a failure, because the Bible says, "And now these three remain: faith, hope and love. But the greatest of these is love" (1 Corinthians 13:13). Love never fails!

On the other hand, you may succeed in climbing to the top of your profession, you may achieve earthly fame and fortune, but if you end up without love, what do you have? A lonely apartment and a telephone that never rings.

I locked the door to my office. Never had I felt so low as I did when I turned my back on the door of my broken dreams. I walked slowly to the parking lot, got into my car and headed for home. Oh, God, it was all I had! I stepped into the house. I expected to hear my wife call out, "Is that you, dear?" I heard nothing. I walked to the kitchen and found a note: "I've gone shopping. Be home late." I sank into a chair, a crushed human being.

Suddenly, the door opened. It was my little girl, home from school. She put her lunch box on the table, spotted me and called, "Daddy! How come you're home so early?" I answered, "Well, honey, daddy is changing jobs, but let's not talk about it now, okay?"

Then my daughter jumped on my lap, hugged me tight around the neck, pressed her warm face against my face, and gave me the warmest, sweetest kiss, saying, "Oh, daddy, I love you so much!" That did it! I really cracked up, my lips quivered. She said, "What's wrong, daddy?" I said, "Nothing, honey, nothing at all. There's absolutely nothing wrong!"

And I really meant it! In that moment I discovered that I had what I really wanted. Suddenly my whole life unfolded before me: the young fellow who wanted to make it to the top in order to be recognized, in order to feel important, in order to be loved, in order to really respect myself! Well . . . I had what

> I wanted . . . It was there on my lap! I was loved!
> And in loving and being loved, I found my sense of
> worth, self-respect and self-dignity!

This wonderful story from Dr. Robert Schuller's book *Self-Love* reminds us what is really important in life: "Let love be your greatest aim" (1 Corinthians 14:1 TLB).

We all have goals in life—things we aim for day by day. Sometimes we shoot for the wrong goal, though, spending all our time and effort on making it to the top. After all, through its films, books, and heroes, society tells us our goal should be to make it to the top. Some people liked the movie *Top Gun* so much that they almost became obsessed with it. I have a friend who has seen it more than a dozen times. A book titled *See You at the Top* enjoyed enormous sales. Once every four years we are glued to our seats in front of the TV by the Olympics, while athletes from all over the world struggle to reach the top and the gold medal. As much as we like to see people go for the gold, there is a penetrating question we need to ask: Is anything more important than making it to the top?

The greatest Book ever written, the Bible, answers this question by telling us, "Yes, there *is* something more important. *Love* is more important than making it to the top." To keep any relationship alive, put love at the top of your list, not work. Without love, you are nothing, I am nothing, and the world is nothing. If it were possible to sum up the teaching of Christ in one word, that word would be *love*.

The Apostle Paul began 1 Corinthians 13 by stating that without love, a person is nothing. If a person is nothing, he is a nobody, the opposite of a somebody, and a nobody is of no worth to himself or anyone else. Life seems most valuable to me when I have love; I feel the strongest feeling of self-worth when I am giving and receiving love.

> **Love is exhilarating! Not only does it make me feel the best but it also brings out the best in me.**

You Have to Work at Love

In America we know a lot about romance, but we know practically nothing about love. Romance can attract people to each other, but it can't keep them together. The headiness of romance lasts a short time, then it's gone. No relationship can endure and have any quality unless it moves beyond romance into love. How does this happen? What makes the difference between a flash-in-the-pan infatuation and lifelong love? And where should we go to learn how to *really* love ourselves and others?

To have true love, we first need to come to God. To learn about love, we first need to go to the Scriptures. To have love at work in our lives, we have to work at it, practice it, and make it our number-one goal. The Bible says it this way: "Therefore, as God's chosen people, holy and dearly loved, clothe yourselves with compassion, kindness, humility, gentleness and patience. Bear with each other and forgive whatever grievances you may have against one another. Forgive as the Lord forgave you. And over all these virtues put on love, which binds them all together in perfect unity" (Colossians 3:12–14).

"Falling in love" is easy, but staying in love requires hard work. As we work at it, love grows and becomes more beautiful. Many people never know a true abundance of love because they stop working on it long before the harvest comes in, running off to another field—hopefully one with no weeds! Pulling weeds is no fun, but in the long run it's easier and more rewarding than clearing a new field and readying it for cultivation.

I enjoy the story of a man who had, some might say, a peculiar habit. For years he had a special date with his wife every Friday night. He would come home in the afternoon, shave and shower, put on his best clothes, go outside, walk around the block, come back, and ring his own doorbell. His wife would greet him at the door. They would sit for a few minutes in the living room and talk, and then they would go out for dinner together. Later in the evening, they would drive up to the front of the house. He would escort her to the door, put the car in the garage, then come in through the back door.

Maybe this sounds a little silly, but let me tell you, when this man died, his wife watered his grave with her tears. She really loved him—because he had *worked* at it!

Love will bring us together!

- to struggle together
- to work together
- to overcome together
- to be together
- to cry together
- to build together

If your marriage is suffering and you are thinking about giving up on it, you are probably looking for any help you can find. You can talk to your family and friends, you can seek professional help, you can read some of the good books out there. They can all help, if you'll let them, but don't overlook your most important asset: your love of God.

The greatest Book on life ever written gives us this rule for a successful marriage: " 'Love the Lord your God with all your heart and with all your soul and with all your mind.' This is the first and greatest commandment. And the second is like it: 'Love your neighbor as yourself' " (Matthew 22:37–39).

> **Loving God first—foremost, intensely, above all else, in spite of anything and everything— is the most important thing you can do.**

If you love God this way, you will find it possible to rebuild your marriage, not throw it away.

Many people lead troubled lives because they don't love God with all their hearts, minds, and souls. They may give lip service to the idea, but they don't really put their love for God first in their lives. If your life is in confusion right now, remember who the author of confusion is. It is not God—it's Satan!

Why do some people come through a crisis victoriously while others come undone at the seams? I believe you'll find the answer to that in the reality of their love for God. When your heart is right with God, when you are yielded to Him and loving Him in spite of anything and everything, He will bring you through it. Sooner or later, you will rise to the top like cream.

On the other hand, if your heart is rebellious and angry, if you insist on doing your own thing, you are not loving God. You have exalted yourself above God and become a little god unto yourself. While denying your Creator, you have worshiped lesser things; your heart is not right with God.

Peter had this problem. After he denied his Lord, his heart wasn't right with God. After the Resurrection, Jesus came to Simon Peter in love, drew him off to the side at the seashore, and asked him right out, "Simon son of John, do you truly love me more than these?" (John 21:15).

Jesus wants to know what's in *your* heart. Do you love Him? How much? Do you love Him enough to put Him first no matter what?

Do you love Him enough to put aside your sexual sins? It's amazing how many people commit sexual sin and rationalize that it is okay. It's not okay! It's against Holy God. How can you say you love God and live immorally? The Bible tells us to flee sexual sins.

"Do you truly love me more than these?" Do you love Jesus more than you love your money? When God gets your heart, He gets your money. Do you love Him enough to give Him the tenth that belongs to Him?

"Do you truly love me more than these?" Some people love the grudge they are holding onto more than they love God. If you love God, you've got to let go of that grudge. The grudge is not helping your relationship with the Father; it is separating you. To love God is to let go of all grudges and give them over to God.

"Do you truly love me more than these?" Do you love Jesus more than you love running your own life? The Bible says, "Love . . . is not self-seeking" (1 Corinthians 13:4, 5). The term *self-seeking* characterizes most people in our world today. Self-seekers want what they want when they want it. Self-seekers use whomever they can to get what they want. The answer to this very destructive problem is to lose yourself in loving God with all your heart. The beautiful thing about doing this is that as you lose yourself in Him, you will find yourself liberated from the need to be self-centered, and when this happens, you are able to show your love for others.

Do you love Jesus so much that you don't compare yourself with others? In the intimate conversation between Peter and Jesus recorded in John 21:15–22, there is a section that I find very humorous because it's so typical of us human beings. Peter turned and saw John, the beloved, then asked Jesus, "Lord, what about him?"

Jesus cut right through all that fussing around about what other people do and don't do. He cut right through the stupid comparison game. He said, "What is that to you? You must follow me" (John 21:22). For your life to straighten out and be filled with love, you've got to get your eyes off other people and follow Jesus. Love God with all your heart, mind, body, and soul.

The Time to Love Is Now!

In *Mourning Song*, Joyce Landorf tells this story:

> I remember an old man at Los Angeles International Airport who broke my heart over his regrets. We were both waiting to board a jet to Hawaii. The man was just sitting beside me when, out of the corner of my eye, I noticed he was very silently sitting there crying. I was about to ask him if I could help when a man on the other side of him did it for me.
>
> The old man just shook his head *no* and continued to cry. When he got a firmer grip on himself, he began talking—not to anyone in particular, but out loud as to why he was on his way to Hawaii. He told about his wife nagging him for thirty years about taking a Hawaiian vacation. . . .
>
> He had firmly said *no* and had given her his reasons. After all, Hawaii held no interest for him and he didn't see any point in going all that way and paying all that money to see an island or two.
>
> Then he said, "Six months ago she got cancer and now—now she's gone." His tears were streaming down his face, but he made no move to dry them. He just continued, "Before she died she made me prom-

ise I'd go and take that vacation in Hawaii for her—so here I am alone—going to Hawaii. God, why didn't I take her when we had all that time and all those years?"

> **Make love your number-one aim. The time to take the time to love is *now*!**

Thinking About Love

1. In the opening part of 1 Corinthians 13, what does Paul say a person is without love? What's your life like without love? How can you get your life back into balance, or on track, according to 1 Corinthians 14:1 (TLB)?

2. What is the most important to you, profit or relationships with people? What gets the most interest in your life—your family members or your work?

3. Fill in the blank: Love grows when we _____ at it. What happens when we don't do this?

4. When it comes to a successful life and learning how to love, what is the heart of the matter, according to Matthew 22:37? Describe a person who has a right heart toward God. Describe a person whose heart is not right toward God.

5. What does the Bible mean in 1 Corinthians 13:4, 5 when it says, "Love . . . is not self-seeking"? What happens to people when they are self-seeking? How does that affect their relationships? What is the cure for this problem?

6. List some of the things people tend to love more

than they love Jesus (*see* John 21). Do you love Jesus more than any of these things? If not, talk to the Lord about what it is that you love more than Him.

7. In Colossians 3:14 we are told, "And over all these virtues put on love. . . ." List the things that we are to do to help us put love into action.

2
Love or Perish

About now you may be saying, "Sure, love is great, and I want it. It makes life enjoyable. But I don't know about making it my number-one goal in life. Lots of people live without it, and I could, too. Couldn't I?" Maybe you can physically live without love, but there's more than one way to die, and do you really want to live out your days feeling dead inside?

Today millions of people are perishing from a variety of diseases of mind, body, and soul because they are trying to live without love. Have you noticed how hostile people are while driving their cars these days? If you look at them cross-eyed, they act as if they'd love to kill you. Anyone that angry is sick!

The famous psychologist John Hunter knew what anger could do to his heart: "The first scoundrel who gets me angry will kill me," he said. Sometime later, at a medical meeting, a speaker made an assertion that angered Hunter. He jumped to his feet, bitterly attacked the speaker, then had a heart attack and dropped dead. We have all heard people say, with clenched teeth, "I'll get that skunk, if it's the last thing I do." Too often it comes to exactly that! Countless people today are making themselves sick over things that don't count. They suffer from heart attacks, indigestion, ulcers, high blood pressure, insomnia, guilt—even mental illness—because they let things get to them. Their priorities are wrong, and it is slowly killing them.

Jealousy, envy, rage, anger, resentment, and hate are all negative emotions that we now know can actually produce disease. They not only make others sick of us, they make us physically ill. Isn't it interesting that every one of these disease-producing negative emotions is concerned with protecting and coddling the self? You see, selfishness makes us sick. Hundreds of years before modern medicine knew anything about psychosomatic illness, the Bible said that negative emotions make people sick. The cure—the antidote—is love. *We must love or perish.*

Without love, we operate out of hate. Instead of respect and good feelings toward others, we have contempt and ill will toward others. You can't build any kind of lasting relationship on hate. Here are some ways that we express our hatred:

- criticism of others
- name-calling
- stubbornness

- snubbing other people
- pouting and demanding our own way
- withdrawing
- wasting energy trying to get even

We pay a heavy price for acting this way. On a trip to Yellowstone Park, Dale Carnegie visited the place where grizzly bears were fed. He did not have to wait long before a grizzly bear came into a clearing where garbage had been dumped to entice him. The guide told the group that the grizzly bear can whip any animal in the west, with the possible exception of the buffalo and the Kodiak bear.

As Carnegie sat with the other tourists in the bleachers, he noticed that the grizzly would allow only one animal to eat with him—a skunk. He no doubt resented the skunk and yearned to get even with him, but he didn't. Why? *Because he knew there would be a high cost for getting even!*

Smart grizzly! He was certainly much smarter than some human beings who spend weary days and sleepless nights brooding over their resentments and trying to hatch ways to get even. The high cost of trying to get even is a variety of diseases of mind, body, and soul.

> **No negative emotion is worth holding on to when you consider what it is doing to you.**

Without Love, Life Is an Ugly Scene

In my book *Rebuild Your Life,* I related this true story:

The phone rang in the home of high-society Boston. On the other end of the line was a son who had just returned from Vietnam and was calling from California. His folks were the pseudo-cocktail circuit, wife-swapping party kind. The boy said to his mother, "I just called, Mother, to tell you that I want to bring a boy home with me. But, Mother, there is something that you need to know about this boy. One leg is gone, one arm is gone, one eye is gone, and his face is quite disfigured. Is it all right if I bring him home?"

His mother said, "Bring him home for just a few days." The son said, "You didn't understand me, Mother. I want to bring him home to live with us." The mother began to make all kinds of excuses about embarrassment and what people would think . . . and the phone clicked.

A few hours later the police called from California to Boston. The mother picked up the phone again. The police sergeant at the other end said, "We just found a boy with one arm, one leg, one eye, and a mangled face, who has just killed himself with a shot in the head. The identification papers on the body say he is your son."

Without love, what do we have? Nothing but one ugly scene after another!

Without Love, I am Beaten!

- I cannot raise emotionally healthy children
- I cannot build a happy marriage

- I cannot be a fulfilled and emotionally whole person
- I cannot mend broken relationships
- I cannot enjoy good feelings about myself
- I cannot cultivate and maintain warm friendships
- I cannot enjoy good health

Without love, I am a lonely, miserable, beaten person. Without love, I have nothing!

Man's heart has an unquenchable thirst for love. Nothing else satisfies. To be loved is the most desperate of human needs.

A successful psychiatrist talked about our greatest need today. He said, "In my practice, people sometimes ask me what psychiatry is all about. To me, the answer is increasingly clear. Almost every emotional problem can be summed up in one particular behavior: it is a person walking around practically screaming, 'For God's sake, love me!' " *Love me*—that is all. Those of us who care about people and observe them carefully see them going through a hundred different manipulations to get somebody to love them.

Without love, what do you have? The Bible says it so well: ". . . faith, hope and love. But the greatest of these is love" (1 Corinthians 13:13).

You cannot even survive without love, let alone be a success in your life!

Love Is the Antidote

Who needs love? No one questions a child's need for love, but parents need love, too. You never get too old to need love. Grandma and Grandpa need love; married people need love; single people need love; pastors need love.

We have to be brave enough to admit this to ourselves and others, like the little girl whose class of sixth-graders went on a field trip to look through a telescope at the stars. She commented, "Teacher, I wish I were a star!"

"Why, child?" the teacher asked.

"Because they are lucky. Those stars are ever so lucky."

"What makes you think so, child?"

"Because Teacher loves those stars," came the reply.

Few adults would be so open as to admit their hunger for love, and yet being loved is the most desperate of all human needs. Who needs love? Everyone! You need it; I need it!

God's Limitless Love

In Portland, Oregon, we have a very fine transportation system. One of our dedicated church members drives a Tri-Met bus. Recently, he was driving in downtown Portland in the northwest section of the city. When he stopped at the bus stop, he was met by a bum.

The bum was unshaven and dirty. When my friend the bus driver opened the door, the odors coming from the smelly bum hit him full force. He said he was thinking, *I hope this bum doesn't want to ride on this bus.*

The bum asked the Tri-Met driver if his bus was going to Vancouver, Washington. The driver was happy to reply that it wasn't. But to his dismay, the bum proceeded to get on the bus anyway. He didn't pay his fare, but the bus driver, not wanting to get into a hassle, didn't say anything to him.

The bum was the only rider on the bus.

When the driver stopped in North Portland, a blind man got on the bus. The blind man didn't see how unkempt and dirty the bum was. He went immediately to where the bum was sitting and sat down beside him.

The bum and the blind man were the only two riders on the bus. The blind man quickly introduced himself: "Hello, my name is Jim." He stuck his hand out to the bum and shook his hand. The bum introduced himself and they had a friendly conversation. As the bus driver listened, his interest intensified when he heard the blind man begin to talk about Jesus. With great love and compassion, the blind man led the bum step-by-step into receiving Jesus Christ as his own personal Lord and Savior. Right there on the bus, they prayed together and the bum became a new person in Christ!

When he was able to stop the bus, the driver went back and had the joy of praying with the blind man and the new child of God. It was a jubilant, happy celebration.

Ten minutes later, at another stop along the route, the blind man and the new Christian got off the bus together and went arm in arm to a Bible study. As they got off the bus, the driver asked God to help him be more perceptive, loving, and to look past the "dirt" in people's lives and see them as people Jesus loves.

To love God's way is to love unconditionally. The love of Jesus is something beyond description.

Oh, how Father God loves you and me! In spite of all the garbage, all the stuff in your life that stinks, Father God wants to take you in His arms and treat you like His favorite child.

God's love is without limit!

Right now, I am writing to someone who has been planning an affair. Your mate doesn't know about it, but you know about it, and you have so many mixed-up feelings. You feel crummy about yourself. You're all confused. Let me tell you this: Father God, in spite of all the garbage in your life, puts His arms around you through Christ and loves you.

Someone else reading this has been involved in one-night stands. You hate yourself for it. You feel ugly. Father God puts His loving arms around you and says, "My child, come on home. I want to forgive you and restore you and give you all My love." When you look at the cross and see the blood of Jesus being poured out, you see exactly how ugly your sin is. It broke the heart of God. But the other truth is that He loves you and me so much!

Let me tell you something about God's love for you. Look at the following verses:

Jeremiah 31:3: "The Lord appeared to us in the past, saying: 'I have loved you with an everlasting love; I have drawn you with loving-kindness.' " He loves you with an everlasting love.

John 3:16: "For God so loved the world that he gave his one and only Son, that whoever believes in him shall not perish but have eternal life." Freely He gives all His love to you.

Romans 5:8: "But God demonstrates his own love for us in this: While we were still sinners, Christ died for us." He loves you without limits and without conditions—just as you are.

1 John 3:1: "How great is the love the Father has lavished on us, that we should be called children of God! And that is what we are!" Father God lavishes His love upon you.

Love Can Be Yours Right Now!

What our world needs now is love, the one thing that can cure the sickness plaguing our generation. Love can restore the broken. It can mend a broken home. It can bring healing to the minds, bodies, and souls of men and women.

Today's social workers, teachers, counselors, and others are at their wits' end because our society seems so defeating.

But with God, all things are possible. Love can make all the difference in your life.

A young man asked me recently, "What does it mean to be a Christian?"

I said, "First of all, it means to receive God's love into

your life. Receive it, accept it, make Jesus your personal Lord. Second, it means to start giving this love that you have received—that you don't deserve—away to other people in your daily life."

The name of the Christian game is love.

Christianity is not something to be inscribed on walls or blazoned on bumper stickers. It is alive with love that should be shared in the everyday relationships of our lives.

Jesus said that the proof of the pudding whether or not we are His followers is this: "A new command I give you: Love one another. As I have loved you, so you must love one another. By this all men will know that you are my disciples, if you love one another" (John 13:34, 35).

Recently Dr. James Dobson's radio program featured a guest psychologist who works with children in special education. He told about one of his most enjoyable experiences in working with the Special Olympics:

> It was the four-hundred-forty-yard dash. There was a host of Special Ed boys of various mental and physical handicaps running the race. At three hundred thirty yards two boys were forty yards out in front of everybody else. The race for first was between these two. Then it happened. The one boy tripped and fell. Immediately the other front-runner stopped and picked the boy up. As he did so, the other runners passed them by.

Arm in arm, the two who had been out in front now were far behind. As you guessed, they finished last. But as they crossed the finish line they were anything but losers. On their faces were written smiles of joy as they hugged and as the other contestants welcomed them with open arms and cheered them. It was one of those great moments when everybody won.

Love is the only way that everybody wins.

> ## Love is our greatest possibility.

Today I read these words again: "Let love be your greatest aim" (1 Corinthians 14:1 TLB). My heart responds to that challenge. Yes, Lord, more than the ability to speak, more than having great knowledge, more than making money, more than getting ahead, more than getting people's attention, I want to love Your way!

Love is the greatest. God's kind of love will bring the best out of you. It is your greatest possibility. Therefore, open up wide to receive all of the love God has for you. Become His instrument through which that love flows into others.

Because . . . God's kind of love wins again and again!

Thinking About Love

1. Read aloud John 3:16. What happens to people without love? Make a list of the diseases of mind, body, and soul that people perish from without love.

2. Who needs love? What would our world be like today if everyone put love into practice? Which would you rather have: a bigger house, a larger bank account, a better job, or more love? Why?

3. Read John 13:34, 35. How did Jesus love us? How are we to love one another? Is love an emotion or a decision?

4. Recall an experience in which someone showed you love.

5. If two people in a marriage have fallen out of love, can they fall back in love again? If so, how? If not, why not?

6. In the following four verses, how does Father God love us?

- Jeremiah 31:3
- John 3:16
- Romans 5:8
- 1 John 3:1

7. What relationship in your life could be improved if you were to practice a little more love?

3
Love Can Be Repaired

Last winter our dryer went kaput, so we called the repairman and he came out to take a look at it. After he evaluated the damage, he said it would cost just about as much money to fix the dryer as to buy a new one, so we agreed it would be best to discard the old dryer and buy a new one.

Just this week my wife informed me that the brakes were going on her car, so we consulted another repairman. This time it was a lot cheaper to make the repairs than it would have been to buy a new car.

Many things in our society can be purchased new cheaper than they can be repaired, so we have turned into a throwaway society. Instead of getting something repaired, we just go out and buy a new one. Don't think this attitude hasn't crept into our personal relationships, too! If love breaks down between two people, we have a tendency to throw away the relationship and look for a "good" one. We just aren't willing to spend the time and effort necessary to repair the relationship, so we treat the other person as if he or she were a malfunctioning can opener, call it quits, and go shopping for a new, improved model.

When people are treated like objects—things to be discarded—the value of human life goes down. On the other hand, when we live Christ's way, value others, and treat them as we want to be treated—when we do everything we can to repair relationships—the value of life goes up. Sure, it costs a lot, and it's not easy to do, but it can be done, and when the repairs are complete, you really have something much more valuable than a "new model."

> Repairing a relationship may be a tough thing
> to do, but it's the most rewarding way
> to live life.

Obstacles to Repairing Relationships

As anyone who has tried to repair even a simple machine knows, each repair job has its own set of obstacles. Ever try to do a simple spark-plug change or change your car's oil, only to find that you can't even *reach* the right area? Every hose in the car is in your way, isn't it? Your hands are too big, you don't have the right wrench—it goes on and on. It's frustrating. But eventually you do get the job done, and the old car is just as good as new (well, almost).

Repairing relationships has its problems, too. Sometimes they seem overwhelming. Let's look at some of these obstacles and see how they can be overcome before we discuss the actual repairs, because until you know how to get around them, you can't fix anything.

Damaged Self-Esteem

As I was flying home from Phoenix one night, I found myself seated next to a child psychiatrist. We struck up a conversation, and I told her about some of the ministries we have at New Hope that strive to produce healthy children who love God, others, and themselves.

She said something that shocked me: "I don't think we have even begun to realize the irreparable emotional damage that is being done to many of our children."

I asked her, "How many years of therapy does it take to repair the damaged self-esteem of a child?"

She replied, "I don't know that we can *ever* repair all the damage that has been done."

From the point of view of modern psychiatry, does this mean that people who have suffered damage to their self-esteem as children must go through life without any hope of being healed and restored? I believe God offers more hope than that.

Carolyn Koons grew up absolutely convinced that no one loved her because she wasn't worth loving. At eight years of age, her mother pushed a gun to Carolyn's forehead and said, "Your dad hates you for all the trouble you've caused us. I'd like to kill you, you no good. . . ." Her father constantly verbally abused Carolyn, treating her as an object of hate.

Things weren't much better at school. She remembers that in the sixth grade, at age eleven, she had one very special student teacher. He took her aside and said, "Beneath all that defensive exterior is a good girl—one who I believe can really become someone very special." No one had ever talked to Carolyn like that before. She listened very carefully and decided that maybe she could be a good girl instead of a troublemaker at school.

A little later, Carolyn told the two boys with whom she had been stealing bicycles that she wanted to stop that activity. As she was taking the bicycles back, her regular sixth-grade teacher grabbed her by the arm and told her that she knew Carolyn was the thief, and now she had caught her. She took her in front of the class and gave her a tongue-lashing, telling the entire class that Carolyn was a rotten, bad, no-good girl. Carolyn listened to these exaggerations and untruths and believed them.

At thirteen years of age, Carolyn was riding in a pickup truck with her dad and mom when they suddenly stopped the truck. Her mother announced that the man Carolyn had thought was her father wasn't her father after all. She had been fathered by another man and was unwanted from the very moment of her conception. They both told Carolyn they didn't want her, they never wanted to see her again, and she had to get out of the pickup. Carolyn got out of the pickup with tears streaming down her face and watched her abusive parents abandon her forever.

She went through other abusive living arrangements, finally ending up alone in a little trailer. She went to high school an unloved, unwanted teenager. Then a Christian lady who loved Jesus came to see Carolyn and told her that God loved her and she was special. She didn't believe it, but she liked to hear it, anyway. The woman kept asking her to go to church. Finally, to get rid of the woman, Carolyn went to church. There she made friends with people who loved God and extended that love to include her. They accepted her as she was. There at the church, in that atmosphere of love and acceptance, Carolyn came to know Jesus as her Lord and Savior. As she grew in His love, her damaged self-esteem began to heal, and she grew into a brand-new person—a loved person who was free to love others. Carolyn Koons has been a faculty member at Azusa College for twenty-seven years. She is one of the most popular teachers on campus. Kids love her. She's a fun, loving person to be around.

Over the years Carolyn has taken more than five thousand students to Mexico on missionary tours and outreach programs. One day in Mexico, God brought a nine-year-old boy who was in prison into her life. He was a troubled kid, abandoned. Carolyn took him in, adopted him, loved him, and became the instrument that brought God's love to his damaged self-esteem and restored him as a person of worth and value. Now, at twenty-three, that boy is a college graduate on the road to using his life to God's glory.

Can love be repaired when self-esteem has been damaged? You bet it can! Nothing is impossible with God. His love is the healing power that we all need in our lives. If your marriage is suffering because of low self-esteem, don't give up on repairing it! This is not an impossible obstacle; you can overcome low self-esteem. Follow these three steps and see what a difference they will make in your life.

Accept God's Love. God's love is for you—right now, wherever you are. Accept it. Keep on accepting it. Let it flow through your whole past, present, and future. Believe this verse: "How great is the love the Father has lavished on us, that we should be called children of God! And that is what we are!" (1 John 3:1).

> **Accept your place as an accepted, loved child of God.**

Think about yourself differently. For years, Carolyn Koons was told a lot of things about herself that were exaggerations or untruths. For a good part of her life, she believed them, and they wiped out her self-esteem. Over the years, you have been told many things that are exaggerations or untruths about you, too. It's time you rethink your views about yourself. Begin by learning what God thinks about you. Realign your thinking with His thinking. He thinks of you as a very special, unique person of great value. He knows that you have faults and weaknesses. So what? Everybody does. All He asks is that you build on your strengths and work on your weaknesses.

Lose yourself to find yourself. Jesus continually taught that the way to find yourself is to lose yourself in Christ and His way. In Galatians 2:20, Paul gives his testimony of how he found his true, lovable self: "I have been crucified with Christ and I no longer live, but Christ lives in me." I paraphrase this to say, lose your unlovable self in Christ and discover your true lovable self.

Imagine a building with only two rooms. One of the rooms is lined with mirrors; the other is lined with windows. In the mirrored room, we can only see ourselves. In the other room, we see the great world around us, filled with people we need and people who need us. It is very important which room we choose to live in. The person who lives in a room with windows gives of himself to Christ and others and ends up truly finding himself!

Selfishness

Another obstacle to repairing love is selfishness. When they first married, this couple appeared to be matched in heaven; they seemed so very much in love. Two kids and six years later, their marriage was coming apart at the seams. They had an adversary relationship, their actions reminding me of a comic strip I saw that showed two Stone Age women conspiring: "I'll tell you what we'll do. We'll roll over and play dead and let them think they are boss. Then we'll nag the suckers into submission." Not only had the wife become a nagging, self-centered, demanding, selfish person, but her husband had bought into the selfish life, too, doing what he wanted whenever he wanted to do it, no matter who it hurt.

When people in a marriage choose to live the selfish life, they always end up being adversaries instead of friends and lovers. This puts up difficult barriers that prevent the relationship from being repaired.

Can love be repaired in a marriage where two people are so egocentric that they have become adversaries instead of lovers? Not unless there is change. Lots of people today are choosing to live the selfish life. The fallout is loneliness and many diseases of mind, body, and soul.

Do you think this couple's choice to live the selfish life is harming their two children? You bet it is! Their son is so insecure that, even though he is four years old, he still wets the bed every night. Their daughter, who is six and could be at the top of her first-grade class, sits in school and daydreams or cries. When love has been thrown out the window in a marriage because Dad or Mom (or both) have chosen to live the selfish life, the result damages their children, giving them emotional wounds that they must carry throughout life.

Leading a selfish life is a choice, but it's always a choice that leads to self-destruction. This is what Jesus taught us in the story about the prodigal son who left his father's house (*see* Luke 15:11–32). The boy came to his father and said, in effect, "I don't care what anybody says. I just want everything I can get." This is so descriptive of so many people today. The father had to let him go; the boy had made his choice. People do make choices, sometimes the wrong choices, so the boy went off into the far country and squandered his wealth in wild living. He spent everything he had. He'd given up his family, he'd lost his self-respect, and he ended up in the pigpen of life—alone, with nothing left. Can love be repaired? Not as long as people choose to be selfish and run away from God.

Bitterness

Clinging to bitterness is another way to prevent a damaged marriage from healing. The prodigal son's elder brother couldn't become reconciled with him after his return because he refused to deal with his bitterness. He was resentful and angry at his younger brother for what he had done to the family's name. He was angry at the father for welcoming the prodigal back. In the end, his sin was worse than his brother's, because his sin was never admitted.

Are you clinging to bitterness over the way your spouse has treated you in the past? Let it go! Anything inside you that separates you from another person is sin. Anything inside you that keeps you from repairing love is sin. Bitterness is just a more subtle form of the old selfishness problem. The Bible warns us, "See to it that no one misses the grace of God and that no bitter root grows up to cause trouble and defile many" (Hebrews 12:15).

Maybe you're saying, "But you don't know what that

person did to me!" The question is not what someone else did or didn't do. The question is, do you have bitterness within you that defiles you and makes you unclean? If you do, confess it right now for the sin it is. Ask Jesus to forgive you, cleanse you, and set you free from it.

How to Repair a Relationship

When the selfish prodigal son hit bottom, what did he do? Did he just wallow there and give up? No! He went to work on his relationship with his father; he healed it. He took seven very hard but necessary steps—steps you can take to heal a damaged marriage, too. Let's look at what he did.

Realization

"He came to his senses" (Luke 15:17). He realized that life wasn't any good where he was. Life had been much better at his father's house. As you read this right now, you may need to come to the realization of where you are. You never dreamed that the selfish life would lead you down this far. Stop playing the blame game and accept responsibility for your relationship. You got yourself where you are by your own selfish choices. Realize that and start back.

Resolution

"I will set out and go back to my father" (v. 18). The prodigal made up his mind that he was going to do something. Hasn't the time come for you to resolve to do what you can to repair your damaged relationship? If you do nothing, nothing will be repaired—it will only get worse. Make a choice to act.

Repentance

"Father, I have sinned against heaven and against you. I am no more worthy to be called your son; make me like one of your hired men" (vv. 18, 19). I want you to look at those words, *make me*. How far is it back to Father's house? How far is it to repairing your love? It is exactly the distance between saying, "give me" and "make me" (*compare* v. 12 with v. 19).

In counseling, when I am working with a couple beginning to accept responsibility for what they have done wrong—a couple that decides to stop playing the blame game and learn to become better people—I know I have the necessary ingredients for healing that marriage.

> **Your love can be healed if you will repent.**

Return

"So he got up and went to his father" (v. 20). For your relationship to be repaired, you have to return to it and do something to straighten it out. You have to swallow your pride and do what's right. The Bible says that God gives grace to those who are humble. Take the grace God offers you, swallow your pride, and return to save your relationship.

Reconciliation

"His father saw him and was filled with compassion for him" (v. 20). God is ready and eager to help with reconciliation. Often before we can be reconciled with another person we need to be reconciled with God. In Luke 15, we see the waiting father with his arms open. He runs and throws his arms around the son, kisses him, and welcomes him home. God the Father is ready to reconcile with you right now, to receive you into His loving arms and forgive you of all sin. Then you will be ready to be reconciled with those you have hurt.

Here is an example of what we are to do for others who have wronged us: We are to throw our arms around them, welcome them back, and be reconciled. We are never more like Jesus than when we forgive one another. Forgive the person who hurt you. Welcome him or her back into your life with open arms, no matter what has been done to you in the past.

Restoration

"Bring the best robe and put it on him" (v. 22). The prodigal was fully restored as a son. Jesus Christ is in the business of bringing about restoration and healing. How wonderful is the healing love of Jesus in our lives! If you and your spouse have been living as strangers, restore your relationship as husband and wife. Give each other the honor due; respect each other and restore your life as a reconciled couple.

Rejoicing

"For this son of mine was dead and is alive again; he was lost and is found" (v. 24). So they began to celebrate. Every time a person comes to God, is reconciled, and becomes a brand-new child of God, it is time for a celebration. Every time, as God's children, we take the initiative and become ministers of reconciliation, repairing broken relationships, it is time for a celebration.

I heard someone tell this moving story: A young man in a midwestern city decided to leave home. He announced his intentions to his father and advised him that he would be leaving the next morning. "I am tired of your restraints and mother's pity," he said.

The night was long and restless for that father and mother. They loved their son and were afraid of what might happen to him in a large city without their Christian counsel. All night they turned restlessly, and the stains of many tears were on their pillows.

The next morning, they heard their son tiptoeing down the stairs an hour before he usually arose. The father jumped out of bed, went to the head of the stairs, and called out to the boy, who had already reached the front door. "Son, come in here a moment!" The boy turned back and walked slowly to his parents' room. His father put his arm gently but firmly around the boy's shoulder and said, "Son, your mother and I have not slept all night. We are sure that there must be something wrong in our lives, and before you go, we want to ask you to forgive us."

The boy looked into the weather-beaten face of his father and saw the tears of love on his cheeks. "Father," the boy said, "the trouble is not with you and mother. The trouble is with me." Together they knelt by the bed and prayed. The boy got up with God's love flowing in his life. After that, home was the happiest place in the world for him.

> **Love will bring you together**
> **and keep you together.**

Don't be afraid. Let go. Openly express your love for one another. I love to go home at the end of the day. To me it's the loveliest, huggiest place on earth! Every morning when I leave and every evening when I return, there is hugging and kissing. This doesn't mean we always see eye-to-eye, that things are always rosy, or that there are never times of misunderstanding. We are imperfect people, learning to live together God's way, but the sun never comes up or goes down without the Galloways touching and in some way expressing their love for one another. The truth is, I can afford no more failures in love. I have had all I want of that in my lifetime. I am determined, with God's help, to live out His marvelous love in our home. Because you have failed in the past or are failing now doesn't mean you cannot succeed!

Thinking About Love

1. What do you think is hardest, repairing a relationship or discarding it and living with the consequences?

2. Can love be repaired when self-esteem has been damaged? If so, how? Jesus talked about losing yourself to find yourself. What do you think He meant?

3. Can love be repaired when a person chooses to live the selfish life? What does selfishness do to a marriage? to a parent-child relationship? to a friendship?

4. What did the prodigal son say to the father that tells us he was choosing the selfish life? (*See* Luke 15:12.) What can we do when people make the wrong choices? What does the Father do when we choose wrongly?

5. Can love be repaired when we act like the older brother and cling to bitterness? Why not? (Read Hebrews 12:15.) What are we to do if we have bitterness inside?

6. According to 2 Corinthians 5:18, what kind of ministry is each of us to have as a Christian? What did Jesus tell us to do in the Sermon on the Mount (Matthew 5:23, 24) that is even more important than praying?

4
You Are Worth Loving!

I want to ask you a very important and personal question, the answer to which will determine the success of your relationships: What do you think and feel about yourself as a person? Before you can make love your number-one aim, you have to believe you are worth loving, or nothing you try will work. What you feel about yourself affects every relationship of your life; your self-concept follows you everywhere. Let's look at five things you really need to know about yourself.

Five Things You Need to Know

You've Got to Discover Your Own Worth and Value

Someone has said that successful people believe in their own worth, even when they have nothing but a dream to hang onto. Why? Because their self-worth is stronger than others' rejection or acceptance of their ideas.

When Walt Disney first started to create and share his cartoon characters, they were rejected. When he was trying to start Disneyland, he had difficulty getting backers who believed enough in his idea to invest in it. Was Walt Disney a better man after he had made a success out of Disneyland than he was when he was broke? Of course not! He was a man of tremendous worth and value *long before* the world recognized him.

Value is in the doer, not the deed.

True worth is not to be found in becoming king of the hill. Do you remember playing King of the Hill when you were a kid, seeing who could knock the others off and stay on top of the highest point? The only problem was, somebody eventually knocked you off. When your dreams are dashed and things don't work out, does that make you a less valuable person? Not if your value and worth come from who you *are* instead of what you *do*.

Worth and value are not to be found in the comparison game. The more you compare yourself with others, the more unhappy you become with yourself. God didn't create you to be like anyone else; He created you to be you. Trying to be like someone else is trying to be second-best. You were never created to imitate someone else; you were created to be the best *you* that you can be.

True value and worth are not to be found in competition. Competition has its place in games and sports, but wise are they who learn to compete only with their previous best, not with others. For example, as a pastor, I am not in competition with pastors in other churches in our city. I only want to do a better job than I did last year.

On more than one occasion, Jesus found a competitive spirit harming the love relationship and self-esteem of His disciples. One time James and John asked to be given the top positions right next to Jesus in the Kingdom (*see* Matthew 20:20–28). This made the other disciples angry. Why were they angry? Because they wanted the position themselves! They wanted to be somebodies.

Jesus took this occasion to teach that being a somebody does not come from being over other people but from giving one's self in a life of service—from fulfilling one's own calling and destiny in life. Giving yourself in service is the way to find yourself.

If You Don't Love Yourself, Your Neighbor Is in Big Trouble

Here are some characteristics of low self-esteem that cause us to have difficulty loving our neighbors:

- Touchiness. Being oversensitive and reactionary.
- Jealousy. Being jealous of another person's accomplishments.

- Inferiority. Feeling inferior to others, which creates the need to try to bring others down.
- Overworking. Having to prove your worth by working all the time instead of taking time to relate warmly to others.
- Smothering. Having to possess someone completely and control him or her because you're afraid you're going to lose him.
- Cheapness. Holding back yourself or money instead of sharing with others.
- Holding grudges. Not forgiving or accepting responsibility for what has gone wrong in the relationship.

Denis Waitley, a well-known motivational speaker and writer of success principles, tells a story in *Seeds of Greatness* about a dog called Buckwheat. Buckwheat was a cute little fellow with beautiful long hair that needed to be brushed every day. He belonged to a little girl named Natalie and her parents. Buckwheat is an example of how low self-esteem changes and damages us.

When Buckwheat's owners moved into a new home in Arizona, they put in a swimming pool to take advantage of the climate. They planted what was to be a large green lawn around the pool and installed underground sprinklers. Buckwheat couldn't keep his nose out of anything. He kept falling into the pool and would either climb out or have to be fished out. Then he would shake furiously to dry off and roll in the fertilizer on the new lawn. When Natalie tried to brush his matted hair, he would yelp and snap at her, though ordinarily he was a friendly dog.

One day Natalie's brother, Nathan, was washing the pool with a long hose and lost hold of it. Buckwheat came to the rescue and charged into the water, growling and biting the enemy.

After the battle he rolled in the fertilizer, which soon looked like the center of a football field in the fourth quarter on a rainy day. Buckwheat looked as if he had played center on the losing team. His mud-tangled coat was beyond repair. Later, at the dog-grooming clinic, the prognosis was what the family had feared—Buckwheat's hair was terminal. It took three people to hold him down during the operation, which consisted of shaving him almost to the skin.

The reception back home was not what little Buckwheat had expected. When he was carried in, the kids made fun of him because he didn't look like a beautiful dog anymore. He now looked like a giant rat. Buckwheat reacted to the teasing and to his new appearance by hiding under the living room sofa. Instead of jumping on everybody's lap, licking every available face, he kept out of sight.

You see, when Buckwheat lost his beautiful coat, he lost more than beauty. The laughter made him shrink and hide away, feeling worthless. Buckwheat's self-esteem plunged to zero. Do you sometimes feel like Buckwheat?

One of the world's best-kept secrets is this:

> ## We must feel loved
> ## before we can give love to others.

This is why Jesus said that we must love our neighbor as ourselves. Another way of putting this is, before we can love our neighbor, we must have some love and acceptance of ourselves. If there is no deep, good feeling of worth inside, if we cannot love ourselves, then we have nothing to give or share with others. A good, healthy dose of self-love is something every bound-up person needs in order to be set free. In Jesus' Name, I want you to be set free to love yourself as a worthwhile person.

Loving Others Does Not Mean Allowing Others to Walk All Over You

In this world, there are users and the used, abusers and the abused. Both extremes are wrong, both are degrading to the person and less than what God created us to be on this earth.

Recently an obviously beaten-down woman came to see me. Her self-esteem was so low that she had difficulty making any decision—for fear, I suppose, that it would be the wrong one. She described how her husband had knocked her around for years. Before her husband's beatings, she had suffered a childhood history of being unloved and unwanted.

For the first time in her life, this woman was beginning to realize that because God loved her, she was a worthwhile person. After listening to the Bible's message about love, she was trying to put this love into practice, so she asked me this question: "Does loving others as Christ loved us mean that I let my husband beat me?"

My friend, to allow another person to abuse you or use you is not love. It is sickness. It is sin.

Jesus said that the greatest commandment is to love God with all our hearts (see Matthew 22:37, 38). The second is to love our neighbors as ourselves. In other words, a Christian is to have three loves: We are to love God, we are to love ourselves, and we are to love others. We are not to have one love or two loves, but all three kinds of love operating in balance in our lives. Each kind of love feeds the others. God's love for us heals us and helps us to build self-love. As we feel good about ourselves, we are able to give love to others. The more love we give to others, the better we feel about ourselves. The more we give healthy love to other people, the more we feel God's love flowing through our lives. What a wonderful feeling it is to be an instrument of God's love by loving others His way!

But loving others does not mean laying down in front of a car and letting it run over you. To a woman abandoned by a husband who had done everything possible to hurt her, I said, "It's time to recognize your own worth emotionally." Allowing another person to keep using and abusing you does not help him. It surely doesn't bless God. Nor does it benefit you in any way, shape, or form.

> You are worth too much as a person of value to allow another person to degrade you and devalue you.

Get Out of the Prison of Self-Centeredness

Self-centeredness and healthy self-love are opposites. People lacking in self-love will keep slipping back into being selfish and self-centered, no matter how hard they try not to. You see, when you are dissatisfied with yourself, you have to keep thinking of yourself all the time. Thinking of yourself as a miserable person locks you into a negative focus. When you are thinking about yourself, you become selfish and hard to live with.

We need a Savior like Jesus to free us from the prison of self-centeredness. His answer? Love God, love yourself, and love others. This is the greatest commandment, the key to successful living (*see* Matthew 22:34–40).

God Thinks You Are Worth Loving

No matter what you think is wrong with you—whatever there is about you that you find unacceptable or unlovable—God believes in you and believes you are worth saving. We read this in Romans 5:8: "But God demonstrates his own love for us in this: While we were still sinners, Christ died for us."

In our generation, the curse upon us is a loss of self-esteem. One of our lay pastors told me that a teenage girl in the high school where she works was ready to commit suicide because she did not feel loved. People are dying from a lack of self-worth and self-love! If you don't feel good about yourself, life is a very lonely trip.

The good news is that Jesus became the curse in our place. He came to take care of our sins, to restore us, to give us forgiveness and healing and all the Father's love. He came to give us salvation, to give us back our dignity and worth, to make us children of the Most High.

Think about this truth: If you had been the only person on this earth, Father God would still have sent Jesus to the cross to atone for *your* sins!

One of my favorite stories is about a boy who made his own little boat out of wood. After he had worked long hours and days shaping it and forming it, he held it up and said, "It's mine. I made it." The next day, with exuberant anticipation, he carried his boat to the shore of the lake and sailed it on the clear, blue water. The little boat that was his pride and joy skipped along as the gentle breezes in its sails blew it across the rippling waves.

Then, suddenly, a gust of wind caught the little boat, snapping the string by which the boy held it. Out farther and farther the little boat sailed, until the heartbroken boy, straining his eyes, could see it no more. Sadly the boy made his way home . . . without his boat. That which he had made was gone.

Weeks and months went by. Then one day as the boy passed a toy shop, something caught his attention. *Could it be? Was it really?* He looked closer. It was! There in the display window was his own little boat.

Overwhelmed with joy, the boy dashed into the store to claim his possession. Excitedly he told the owner the boat on display was his. He had made it with his own hands. "I'm sorry," the storekeeper said, "but it's my boat now. If you want it, you will have to pay the price for it."

Disappointed once again, the boy left the store. But he was determined to get his boat back.

At last the day came. Tightly holding his money in his fist, he proudly walked into the shop, spread his hard-earned money on the countertop, and said, "I've come to buy back my boat."

The clerk counted the money. It was the exact amount. Reaching into the showcase, the storekeeper took the boat and handed it to the eager boy. The lad's face lit up with a smile of satisfaction as he held the little boat in his arms. "You're mine," he said, "twice mine. Mine because I made you, and now mine because I paid the price to buy you back."

Not only did God make you special in the beginning, but when you were lost and drifting away from your Maker, He paid the ransom price by sending His Son, Jesus Christ, to die for your sins and buy you back. Without God, man loses his worth and value, but in fellowship with God, man's true worth is restored. The question is, why did God give His Son to buy you back? Because He loves you. God not only sees your sins, He sees beyond them, to your worth and your unlimited potential as He first made you.

> ## God believes you are worth loving!

You mean, even with my sins? Yes!
Even with that which is degrading to look at in myself? Yes!
Even with my faults? Yes!
Even with my shameful past? Yes!
Even with all my failures? Yes!
To you, God says:

> My child,
>> I love you.
> My child,
>> I accept you.
> My child,
>> I care about you.
> My child,
>> I forgive you.
> My child,
>> I am going to use you.

Thinking About Love

1. What does it mean to you personally that God gave you your worth at birth? Read Genesis 1:27–31. What was the psalmist's response to the way he was created? Read Psalms 8 and Psalms 139:13, 14.

2. If you don't love yourself, why is your neighbor in big trouble? What are some of the symptoms of

low self-esteem that cause difficulty in loving one's neighbor?

3. Read Matthew 22:34–40. What three loves are we to have as Christians? How does each of these feed the others?

4. Does loving others mean that you have to allow a person to abuse you or use you? Why do you say so? How does allowing a person to abuse you repeatedly affect self-esteem? How does it affect the person who is allowed to do the using or abusing?

5. How does choosing to live the selfish life affect self-esteem? How are selfishness and self-esteem opposites? How does low self-esteem tend to lock a person in to selfishness?

6. Read Romans 5:8. What did Christ's death on the cross do for our self-esteem? How is poor self-esteem a curse on our generation, and how does Christ's death on the cross deliver us and give us new self-worth and value?

5
Love Is a Choice

So you are willing to admit that you're a worthy person—someone who deserves to be loved as one of God's children. Good! That's the first step on the road back to a restored relationship. From now on, repairing a relationship is to a great extent a matter of choice. There are actions you should or should not take, techniques you can learn, specialists you might want to consult. But all of these are useless unless you make a conscious choice to save the relationship. Once that decision is made, healing is possible.

One of the greatest gifts God has given us is the power of choice. Every day, in many ways, we choose to love or not love. All those choices combine to create the environment of a relationship. When we choose to love, our relationships are healthy. When we choose not to love, our relationships perish.

Always Act in Love

When people choose not to act in love, the results are never good. One of the very first people to live on this earth was Cain, and when he chose not to love his brother, Abel, hate took hold of him and he murdered his brother. Without love, nothing good happens. Scripture says, "Anyone who does not love remains in death. Anyone who hates his brother is a murderer, and you know that no murderer has eternal life in him" (1 John 3:14, 15).

In contrast to this way of destruction is the way of Christ, the way of giving love and doing what Jesus, who "laid down his life for us" (1 John 3:16), did.

> **Love is something you do because it is the right thing to do.**

The Lord Jesus commands us to choose love: "A new command I give you: Love one another. As I have loved you, so you must love one another" (John 13:34).

> **For the person who wants the best in life, love is the only viable choice.**

So often we try to substitute all kinds of other things to keep from doing what we know is right, but no relationship can turn out well until we do what is right with love.

Relate to Others Out of Love, Not Fear

I read a story about an explorer who went to the wilds of Africa. He took a number of trinkets along for the natives, among them, two full-length mirrors. He placed these mirrors against two trees and sat down to talk to some of his men about the exploration.

Meanwhile some of the natives had great fun smiling at themselves in the mirrors. Then one of the natives approached the mirror with a scowl on his face and a spear in his hand. When he looked into the mirror, he saw his reflection and began to jab his "opponent" in the mirror as if it were a real person, going through all the motions of killing him. Of course, he broke the mirror into many pieces.

Seeing this, the explorer walked over to the native and asked why he had smashed the mirror. The native replied, "He go kill me . . . I kill him first."

When we act out of fear, we live far below the abundant life that Jesus came to give us. What are we afraid of? Most of our fears fall into three categories: fear of rejection, loss, or pain.

When we are afraid that we will not be accepted, that we will be rejected, we start withdrawing and trying to protect ourselves. We won't allow other people to get close to us. Living like this imprisons us instead of freeing us.

> **Love frees—fear imprisons.**

The second category of fear is fear of loss. One of the most painful arrays of human emotions is related to our fear of losing something or someone special to us. Trying to protect ourselves from loss, we become possessive, clinging, and demanding. Possessiveness does not rise from love but from fear, and it kills love.

A great lover is one who releases. He is able to release because he has been released.

> **If you love something, set it free. If it comes back to you, it is yours. If it doesn't, it never was.**

The third kind of fear is fear of pain. For example, when we have been hurt in a relationship, fear will make us pull back into our shells and not commit ourselves in a new relationship. Remember this: "God did not give us a spirit of timidity, but a spirit of power, of love and of self-discipline" (2 Timothy 1:7).

Who wants to be paralyzed by fear? To better understand the relationship between fear and love, let's draw a parallel between darkness and light. Let's assume that most of my life I have been living and working in the dark. Not only has it been difficult to be productive, it has been painful and destructive, because I continually bump into and fall over things.

I keep thinking, *There's got to be a better way.* Then somebody tells me I need to get rid of the darkness. But how do I do that? Well, I can get angry at the darkness, spit on the darkness, and punch the dark air with my fist, but it will not go away. None of these actions will bring any change. To my knowledge, there is only one way to banish darkness: Turn on the light.

God is light, and God is love. The more we allow God's light and love to come into our lives, the more we will dispel the fearful darkness.

> **Stand up to the things you fear the most with turned-on love from Jesus, and the death of fear is certain.**

Love Is Something You Do

Love is never passive. You don't just sit there and call out to the world, "Hey, I love you all!" Try that and someone's going to call back, "Oh yeah? What have you done for *me* lately?" Love is active! The only time love becomes visible is when you are doing something that illustrates it.

Recently, Pastor Floyd Schwanz, one of my fellow staff members, met an old friend who told him about the new child in his family. A young mother of seven children had been left widowed. In her grief, she felt all alone and unable to cope with the problems, so she abandoned her children. Pastor Floyd's friend had a large family, but when he heard about these children, his family got together and decided that they would take all seven of the children, with different married brothers and sisters taking one or two of the children. They presented their plan to the court, and of course the court was more than glad to have stable homes for the children.

Once a month they all get together so the brothers and sisters can see one another. The man testified that not only had it blessed his immediate family but that his whole family was being drawn closer in love because of their actions.

The Bible says, "Dear children, let us not love with words or tongue but with actions and in truth" (1 John 3:18). In other words, don't just talk about it; *do it.* Love is being there, doing what needs to be done. It is serving the other person, doing what you can do to meet someone's need. When you act in a loving manner, people will believe you when you declare your love.

Emotions Don't Count

A Professor James once said: "Emotions are not subject to reason, but always subject to action."

Practice love whether you feel like it or not. People who run their lives by their emotions are like a train waiting to be pushed by the caboose. If you sit around waiting until you have good feelings about someone before you act in love toward him or her, you're going to stop love cold! Christian love is not fondness, it's not how you feel, it's what you *do,* regardless of how you feel. You do it not because you feel like it but because it is the right thing to do. Set your will to love someone and your emotions will follow along.

A man I was counseling complained, "I don't love my wife."

I said, "Do you *want* to love her?"

He said, "Come on, you can't *make* yourself love somebody."

My answer was simple: "Of course you can. If you set your mind to act in love, your emotions will follow along. What you do conditions the way you feel. If you do loving things, soon you will have loving feelings. Your emotions are influenced by your actions."

I challenged this man to make a list of ten things he could do for his wife to show her that he loved her—and then to go home and start doing them.

A couple of days later he called and said, "It's wild! I made a list of ten things that I would do for my wife if I loved her. I decided to do those ten things. I got all spruced up the other night and took her out for dinner. I treated her like the most special person in all the world. I gave her some flowers and opened the car door for her.

"About halfway through the evening, she asked me if I was drunk. But what a difference there was in the atmosphere at our home in about two days! I'm beginning to think that maybe I could love her."

A week later the man came back and said he was falling in love with his wife all over again. They were still the same two people. What made the difference?

One of them had decided to act in a loving manner, regardless of how he felt. Do something loving for that person you don't feel like loving, and watch your feelings be transformed.

A woman was feeling really bad because her favorite neighbor had moved, and she was having trouble accepting the people who moved into her friend's house. She decided that she had better take some loving, positive action and change her feelings.

So she made a lemon meringue pie for her new neighbor. When she first started making the pie, she felt kind of ridiculous, but before she finished with it, she was starting to feel much better. She gave her feet a stern look and informed them that they were to carry the pie next door to the new neighbor. She rang the doorbell, and the lady came to the door. As soon as she handed her neighbor the pie, the woman started to feel an accepting, warm feeling for the woman! As the days passed, they became close friends. Plant the seeds of love and you will reap a harvest of love. It may not be easy to take those first steps of love, but they have multiple rewards.

When You Are Wronged

When somebody does something to you that you think is wrong and unfair, stop and ask yourself these important questions:

- Do I want to be like him, or worse?
- Do I want to make this situation worse than it is?
- Do I want to act like a Christian or a non-Christian?

Remember, the only person who can make you act in an unloving, unchristian way is *you!* Only you can decide how you will act. Tell yourself this truth: This emotional crisis is my greatest opportunity, with Christ's help, to show other people what real Christian love is like. Love is something you do no matter what others do.

Several years ago, I read *The Seed Must Die,* by Young Coon Ahn, the story of a Korean pastor who went through the atrocities of the Second World War and was in prison most of his life. When he was released from prison, he and his two sons established a new ministry in Korea. Soon the Communists began their uprising in Korea, which in the early days was more of a student revolution than a military action. During one of the student riots, his two sons were shot by the Communists.

Some of those who were thought to have done the deed were caught and put on trial.

The response from the dear pastor was unbelievable. He wrote to Christian friends in the city where the trial was being held:

> When the people of a country fight against each other, who can tell where it will end? Each side will take revenge on the other, and this could go on until almost all are destroyed. The tide of revenge must be checked. Let someone go at once to Pastor Duk Whan in Soon Chun and tell him those who killed my sons,

if they are found, must not be beaten or put to death. I wish to adopt them as my sons.

One of the boys was found guilty. Only the godly pastor's intervention kept that boy from death at the hands of the angry people. The killer became part of the pastor's family, and the sister of the two martyred brothers became a sister of the man who had killed them. It was almost a year before the boy finally responded and was converted, but at the end of the book is part of a letter the son wrote to his adopted father from a Bible school:

> Please don't be worried about me. I study the Bible, pray, join in the singing, and do some preaching. Please pray for me. I know I owe everything to you— your prayers and others. As your eldest son, I shall use every means of growing in the spiritual life. And, Father, please forgive me for everything. Because of your love given me by God, I shall try to fulfill your desires for me and shall attempt to follow in the footsteps of St. Paul. I shall do all in my power to follow after the example of my two brothers.

It is not God's will for us to live negatively, to retreat and become occupied with our own hurts to the exclusion of all else. Ours is the highest of challenges: to be the salt of the earth, making men thirsty for God's love. Love is your best possibility. As God's own child, you have been chosen to live creatively and positively by putting your love into action. This is your opportunity to bring Christ's love to bear in some of the most distressing situations that life has to offer. Sound impossible? It is! But with Christ we can do all things. We can act in a loving way when we don't feel loving.

> **Love is something you do**
> **no matter what others do.**

I don't know about you, but my greatest desire is to be known as a man who loves. You see, that's what being a Christian means!

Thinking About Love

1. Is love an emotion or an action? Explain.
2. Without love, what takes over in a person's life? What are the results? (*See* 1 John 3:14, 15.)
3. What are some of the ways that fear destroys our love? Try to identify relationships in which you are having difficulty because instead of relating in love you are relating out of

- fear of rejection
- fear of loss
- fear of pain

4. How do you apply these verses to your life in overcoming fear?

- 2 Timothy 1:7
- John 14:18

5. Apply this rule to some relationship you have right now: Love is something you do, no matter how you feel. Now apply this rule: Love is something you do, no matter what others do.

6. How may we have the power to love when we don't feel like it? (*See* Romans 5:5.)

6
Spoiler Attitudes
That Destroy Love

It's not the site or the size that makes a church great, but its spirit. What is this spirit? Love!

It's not where they live or the size of their bank account that makes a family close and happy, but its spirit. What is this spirit? Love!

It's not their likes or dislikes that bring people together and keep them together in friendship, but their spirit. What is this spirit? Love!

We've been saying that without love, people perish from a variety of diseases of mind, body, and soul. At the heart of the Bible is the verse that says, "God so loved the world that he gave his one and only Son, that whoever believes in him shall not perish but have eternal life" (John 3:16). With God's kind of love operating in our lives, we don't just survive, we thrive.

Love lights up our lives!

As much as we all want this type of love in our lives, some of us seem to be pushing it away by our attitudes. We say we love, but our actions say something else. There are ten attitudes that can destroy love. Let's take a look at each of them and learn how to handle them.

Hanging Judge

Jesus warns us against the Hanging Judge attitude in these words from Matthew 7:1, 2: "Do not judge, or you too will be judged. For in the same way you judge others, you will be judged, and with the measure you use, it will be measured to you."

Jesus also taught us to have nothing to do with the Hanging Judge attitude in the eighth chapter of John. The Pharisees were classic examples of the Hanging Judge attitude. They caught a woman in adultery and threw her at Jesus' feet, demanding that she be stoned to death. Of course, they didn't say anything about their own sins.

Jesus said to them, "If any one of you is without sin, let him be the first to throw a stone at her" (John 8:7). Then, speaking to the woman with love, acceptance, and forgiveness, He said, "Then neither do I condemn you. Go now and leave your life of sin" (v. 11).

When I allow the Hanging Judge attitude to creep into

my life, love goes right out the window. Why should a person I condemn love me? If I'm so "far above" everyone, I'm standing all alone, aren't I? I'm certainly not showing my love the way Jesus showed His to the adulteress.

A pastor told this story in one of his sermons:

> One day a minister came to see me, and he was depressed. He said, "I had a funeral yesterday for a beautiful Christian woman.
>
> "When I came to my church, I looked across the membership roll and noticed the name of a woman I had never met. Someone told me she used to be such a faithful worker, but then something happened. 'She stopped coming to church a few years ago, and boy, has she changed! She won't have anything to do with anyone anymore. She is such a snobbish, secretive person! We think it's because she has inherited some money. Those who have stopped over to the house say that she is always lounging around in very expensive, flimsy nightgowns, wearing expensive perfume, and a glass of liquor is always within reach. She watches television constantly, and what's worse, once a week when her husband is at work, a strange man with an out-of-town license plate drives up, goes in, stays about an hour, and leaves. It's a pity the way a good Christian can suddenly go to the devil.'
>
> "Then suddenly one day she died," the minister recalled, "and her husband came to me and asked if I would conduct the funeral. I told him I would but that I thought she was no longer a member of the

church. I told him what I knew about her. The husband was shocked!

" 'My wife,' he explained, 'had an incurable disease that hit her several years ago. She bought perfume to cover the odor, and she only wore flimsy nightgowns so the weight of the clothing would not hurt her abdomen. The liquor was a bonafide medicine. The man coming to see her once a week was a specialist from out of town. She was secretive because she wanted to keep it from the kids, so they would not know they were going to lose their mom. Oh, she was a beautiful Christian all through it, to the end.' "

The minister and his congregation had been acting as Hanging Judges, not the loving, supportive body of Christ they thought they were!

The other day I was reading Romans 8:1, which is a tremendous verse: "Therefore, there is now no condemnation for those who are in Christ Jesus." I have always seen this verse as a great liberator from self-condemnation and self-punishment, and it is. But there is more here. When we are living in Christ, close to Him, there is no room for condemning and judging others.

Love finds a way to get off the judgment seat and get on the mercy seat.

Bragging Brat

You remember hearing little children saying, "My daddy can beat up your daddy," or "My big brother can beat up on you." Pitting ourselves against one another like that destroys love.

In 1 Corinthians 3, Paul talked to the Corinthians about their church's spirit. They had chosen up sides, pitting one leader against another. They were playing the comparison game, using different Christian leaders as their rallying point for competition. Paul said they were acting like babies. This was not God's way for them to live; as God's children, we are not in competition with anyone.

I liked Carl Lewis's maturity and class when, after the Olympics in Korea, reporters kept trying to get him to compare himself with other competitors. They tried it first when he barely got nosed out in the hundred-yard dash. Then they tried again when he got nosed out by a close friend and fellow American in the two-hundred-yard dash. Carl, being a wise person, refused to compare himself with the other competitors. All he would say was that he ran his best. He ran to his fullest potential.

Love is being the best you can be and helping others be the best they can be, all to the glory of God. Love is not telling your wife you wish she'd learn how to cook like your mother. Love is not telling your husband that he makes far less money than his neighbor. Love does not compare.

Rude Dude

Watch out for the attitude of rudeness. It is such a subtle little failing, yet so destructive to relationships.

This is what 1 Corinthians 13:4, 5 (TLB) says: "Love is very patient and kind, never jealous or envious, never boastful or proud, never haughty or selfish or rude. Love does not demand its own way."

Little things like kindness, courtesy, and thoughtfulness mean so much that we cannot afford to forget them. If we do, our relationships begin to suffer. Remember, the little things either tear down or build up a daily relationship. As this poem puts it:

> It's the little things we do or say,
>   That make or break the beauty
>   of an average passing day,
> Hearts, like doors, will open with ease,
>   To very, very little keys.
> And don't forget, that two of these
>   Are "I thank you," and "If you please."

Generally, people don't get divorces because of bad table manners, but they do when one person is habitually rude, unkind, or unfeeling. Small daily snubs add up, until the burden is just too much to bear and the relationship snaps. Meticulous good manners may not be necessary, but common courtesy indicates and deepens love.

Mess Maker

If you want to mess up any good feelings that you have for yourself, just let this Mess Maker creep into your life. If you want to reap destruction in your marriage, let this Mess Maker crawl into your bed. If you want to open yourself up to all kinds of diseases of mind, body, and soul, let this Mess Maker travel from place to place with you.

What is this Mess Maker that wreaks such havoc and is so destructive to love? It is the ugly spoiler of sexual immorality. He is everywhere in our society, killing and destroying love. If you let him into your life, he is going to harm your love for God. He's going to make you feel crummy about yourself. And he is going to hurt the relationships that mean the most in your life.

This is why the Bible says, "Flee from sexual immorality. All other sins a man commits are outside his body, but he who sins sexually sins against his own body. Do you not know that your body is a temple of the Holy Spirit?" (1 Corinthians 6:18, 19).

Treat your body as the temple it is and sexual immorality will have no chance to destroy your marriage.

Sunglass Kid

The Sunglass Kid is always shading the truth. The builders of love are honesty and trust; lying and deception tear down love. You may choose to lie to people because you think you are avoiding pain, but in the long run, deceitfulness always brings more pain because it destroys love.

Romans 12:9 says, "Love must be sincere." In other words, let it be without deceit, without deception. Let it be sincere and straightforward. Dishonesty with those you love only erodes the relationship—perhaps so seriously that it crumbles, damaged beyond repair.

Touchy Tillie

Touchy Tillie wears her feelings on her sleeve. Every time she doesn't get treated as she thinks she's supposed to, she runs off into the corner and hides, expecting everyone to come and give her extra attention. What a childish game of hide-and-seek Touchy Tillie plays. The more we withdraw from other people, the lonelier we get and the less love is in our lives.

> **Open yourself up to others, and they will be drawn to you. Close yourself off from others, and you will find yourself alone.**

Pistol Pete

People stay away from Pistol Pete because they never know when he's going to start shooting. About the time he begins to get close to someone, he erupts in verbal abuse, and everyone runs for shelter. Sometimes Pistol Pete tucks all his unresolved anger inside and holds on to it. Either way, his anger is terribly destructive to himself and his relationships.

Ephesians 4:26 says, "Do not let the sun go down while you are still angry." Get a handle on your anger, admit it, and deal with it. Galatians 5:23 teaches us how to gain control of our lives through the Holy Spirit.

Brick Bat

Bats, as you know, are blind. The Brick Bat is so stubborn that he can't see what he's doing and what is going on around him. He is so set on trying to prove who is right and who is wrong that he allows Satan to rule his life instead of Jesus.

First Corinthians 13 teaches us that love keeps no records of right and wrong. A person in love doesn't have to prove himself smarter or better than the other person. Who cares who's right and who's wrong? Love finds a way to break through, communicate, and find understanding. Remember what it says in Ephesians 5:21 (TLB): "Honor Christ by submitting to each other."

Clinging Vine

When you have this possessive attitude, you want someone to have no other friends but you. You will try to possess the person completely and never let him or her out of your sight. If that person even talks to someone else, you become insanely jealous. Wherever you go, the other person must go with you, clinging like a vine.

Smothering another person destroys love. The Bible says, in 1 Corinthians 13:5 (PHILLIPS), "Love . . . is not possessive." True love sets people free to be themselves.

Hurry-Scurry

This attitude causes neglect. And what is neglect? Being busy hurrying and scurrying everywhere and not paying any attention to your relationship. To grow in love, relationships require attention.

Love is paying attention.

Love Finds a Way

In 1 Corinthians 13, right in the middle of this great love chapter, we are told to grow up and put behind us the childish ways we have called spoiler attitudes so love can grow within us and through our lives. Let's commit ourselves, through the power of the Holy Spirit, to loving others God's way.

In her book *Broken Members, Mended Body*, Kathy Miller tells the following story:

Janet's father died when she was six. Her mother tried to drown her grief in alcohol and men—lots of men—forgetting that her daughter, too, was grieving. Indeed, forgetting about her daughter altogether.

Throughout her childhood and teen years, Janet had difficulty developing and maintaining friendships. What few friends she had, she never brought home with her. She was too ashamed. By her junior year in high school, Janet was starved for love. Before the year was over, she was pregnant. Her boyfriend talked her into having an abortion, then he left her. She never went back to school.

Instead, she found a job as a waitress and continued to live with her mother, although the two of them hardly spoke except to argue. When one of her mother's boyfriends raped Janet, she moved out. She didn't report the rape because she figured no one would believe her, including her mother. She also figured she had probably done something to deserve it.

Janet never saw her mother again. By the time her mother died two years later, Janet was so strung out on drugs that she missed the funeral. She was living with boyfriend number five. She had long since lost her job; they supported themselves by selling drugs. Occasionally Janet sold her favors to one of her boyfriend's buddies. Her boyfriend didn't mind. It was his idea.

When she realized that once again she was pregnant, she told her boyfriend. He called her filthy names, refused to accept responsibility for the child, and left.

Once again, Janet was alone. As she had every day since she was six years old, she felt unloved. The pain was more than she could bear. As she drew the razor across her wrist, the only thing she felt was relief. She woke up in the hospital. She was angry because she had botched the job. She had survived but her baby had not.

There in the hospital she met Sharon, who had come into the hospital because she had cancer. Janet thought Sharon was strange. How could she be having cancer tests and not be scared? Why did she seem so cheerful? Why was she reading the Bible all the time? How weird!

One evening, several of Sharon's friends came to visit her. They were just like Sharon, reading their Bibles, talking about God as if He were right there with them. Janet thought these people were crazy.

LOVE! LOVE! LOVE! LOVE! Janet thought. *Is this all these people ever talk about?* Well, maybe they had love, but she sure didn't know anything about it. What were they doing now? Good grief! It sounded as if they were all praying. Janet peeked over a little bit and watched them. They were talking to God as if He were right there.

"Thanks for coming," called Sharon as they filed out the door. The last to leave was an older woman. As she was leaving, she stopped by Sharon's bed to give her a hug. As she did, she looked over to Janet and said, "Jesus loves you, too." Her smile was warm and something about her eyes touched Janet.

"Wait!" cried Janet. The woman stopped and came back beside Janet's bed. Janet's heart beat faster. She asked the older woman, "Why did you say that?" And right there the New Hope lay pastor explained God's love to Janet and led her to know Jesus personally.

Later Janet testified, "That moment was the first time since I was a very little girl that I really felt loved. That love has literally changed my life for the better."

Thinking About Love

1. Hanging Judge—Read Matthew 7:1, 2 and identify the attitude called Hanging Judge. What happens to love when you start judging another person?

2. Bragging Brat and Rude Dude—What happens to love when you start playing the comparison game? Name someone you have been rude to recently. Read 1 Corinthians 13:4 (TLB) and find out what it says about being rude. List some ways you can be kinder to the people closest to you.

3. Mess Maker—What does immorality do to a marriage and family? to a single person? to one's self-esteem? In 1 Corinthians 6:18, what are we told to do about immorality?

4. Sunglass Kid and Touchy Tillie—What does lying or deceit do to love? What happens if we are always getting our feelings hurt too easily? Does it ever do any good to go off and withdraw from other people? What happens when you hold people responsible for something they don't know about?

5. Pistol Pete and Brick Bat—What does anger taken out on other people do to the relationship? What does anger tucked inside and not dealt with do to us? Is stubbornness a childish attitude or a grown-up one? What does the Bible tell us to do in 1 Corinthians 13:11?

6. Clinging Vine and Hurry-Scurry—describe someone who is possessive of another. How does possessiveness affect love? What happens when we allow others to be themselves? How does neglect affect a relationship?

7
Don't Let the Warts Stop Your Love

How bogged down and defeated we become when we allow ourselves to think about another person's faults! Everything becomes blown out of proportion, and we drive away the very people we so badly need.

For nine long years, Aaron and Debra had wanted a baby. Finally the long-anticipated day arrived, and Debra gave birth to a nine-pound, six-ounce baby boy. He was perfect in every way except that there was a birthmark over his right eye.

When Aaron and Debra saw their firstborn, all they could see was the birthmark over his eye. Debra became so upset and hysterical that she started shouting, "I don't want him! I don't want him! He's got a horrible, hideous mark on him. Take him back."

Can you imagine someone longing to have a baby and then rejecting that baby because he had a little birthmark over his eye? Worse things than this happen when we start centering on one another's imperfections. In the Bible we read this magnificent verse (*see* 1 Peter 4:8):

> "Love overlooks a multitude of faults."

Don't Pick at Another's Weak Spots

In reading an article about turkeys, I learned that when a turkey is wounded and has a spot of blood on its feathers, the other turkeys will pick at that spot until they literally pick the wounded bird to death. When I first read this, my reaction was, "How cruel!" My second thought was, "How dumb turkeys must be, to keep picking at the wound of a fellow turkey."

As a human being, you have the choice of being smart or dumb. You can be smart and refuse to pick at another's wound, or you can be as dumb as a picking, pecking turkey. If picking and pecking is such a dumb thing to do, why would we ever be tempted to do it? People play the picking game in order to build up their own sinking egos. Sometimes we try to make the other guy look bad so we will look better. But the reality is that when we pick, all we do is make ourselves feel crummy. We end up looking worse than the person we're trying to make look inferior. Remember, picking always hurts the picker more than it hurts the picked.

God has a better way for us to live. It's called the superior way of love. Love overlooks a multitude of faults.

Sure, your wife could afford to lose twenty pounds, but does your harping on that help either of you? Would you rather live with her as she is or risk losing her? Sure, your husband watches too much football, but he is home with you. Where would you prefer him to watch the game? Picking at something that can't easily be changed is dangerous, foolish, and never worth the damage it does to love.

Understand That No One Is Perfect

If you can love only perfect people, whom are you going to love?

Not me,
Not any of your family members,
Not anybody you work with,
Not anybody at church.
Not sinners,
and
certainly not yourself!

I remember a woman who said she was going to leave her church and go to another one. When asked why, she said she was looking for a perfect church. The person she told this to confronted her with the fact that once she joined that church, it wouldn't be perfect anymore, because *she* was not perfect.

If you're a perfectionist looking for perfect people to love, good luck! Don't expect me to be perfect, because God is not finished with me yet. I pray that you will be freed from expecting perfection, because you are expecting the impossible. Someone has wisely said, "The seed of discontent is in the expectation."

Often we get all upset at other people because we expect something from them that, first of all, we've never communicated to them and, second, they have never accepted responsibility for. Often employers are absolutely frustrated because the people they employ will not work at the business the way they do. If you're an employer, you have to ask yourself if this is a realistic or unrealistic expectation. People who are not the owners of a business are simply not likely to work the way the owners do. However, if you can communicate realistic expectations to them, they will respond positively.

Don't Major on Minors

Most of the things that upset people are really very minor. We can save ourselves a lot of heartburn by asking one question: Is this really that important?

Once there was a mother who was continually upset by her teenage son's hair, which always looked ragged and was too long to suit her. She constantly badgered him to get his hair cut, because she saw her son's hair as a social embarrassment.

One day when she went to pick up her son after football practice, she viewed a live drama taking place before her very eyes. She witnessed another teenage boy about her son's age and his mother having a fight. The boy shouted ugly words at his mother, showing his utter contempt and disrespect for her in front of everyone. At that very moment, the Christian mother realized what a wonderful son she had—a son who loved and respected his mother. Right there she bowed her head and asked God to forgive her for making such a big thing out of nothing.

> **Love centers on what really counts.**

Get Off the Judgment Seat

In the novel *Not as a Stranger*, Leonard Griffith tells of an episode in which young Dr. March went to the president of the district medical society to accuse an older colleague of malpractice.

The president listened patiently and then asked the younger man to reconsider his charges. He suggested that Dr. March not act hastily, but remember that young men tend to judge more harshly than they do after they have been mellowed by age.

The young doctor remained adamant. The president's

eyes narrowed. His attitude changed. He leaned forward across the desk and said, "I am going to just suggest this to you—that if you persist in bringing formal charges, then be sure of one thing. Don't you, as long as you live, make a single mistake."

To live on the judgment seat is to become a miserable critic, condemning and separating yourself from others. Living on the mercy seat means overlooking, forgiving, giving the benefit of the doubt, going the second mile, and enjoying other people, even when they do things you don't think are right.

How good are you at getting along with people who are different from you? You know that every person alive is different from you and no one else is just like you, so if you have to have people be like you before you can love them, you are not going to love anyone. You are going to be a very lonely, isolated person. I have a friend who has a tremendous capacity for honoring people who disagree with him. He can state his own belief or position very well, yet he always gives the other person the right to have his own viewpoint, and he respects that person. He has a very special way of making friends out of enemies.

If everyone has to agree with you before you will love them, you're in big trouble. If you keep cutting everyone out of your life who disagrees with you, after a while no one will be left to give you love or receive love from you. The person I love the most, my wife, Margi, has opinions of her own, and sometimes they are different from mine. In fact, they are quite often. That does not stop us from respecting and loving each other. Yes, love overlooks differences and appreciates the uniqueness of the other person.

Don't withhold your love from another person simply because of differences. Some people are so exclusive, so narrow-minded, that their ears touch each other. Love never excludes; it always reaches out and includes. Someone has said it so well in this little poem:

> He drew a circle that shut me out,
> Heretic, rebel, a thing to flout,
> But love and I had the wit to win;
> We drew a circle that took him in!

Stop Trying to Change People

When you try to change another person, you are saying to him, "You are unacceptable to me."

One of our greatest needs is to be accepted, and one of the best gifts you can give another person is your acceptance. If you love a person, you want to help him, and the way you help him is not by trying to change him but by accepting that person as someone of worth and value. Treat the other person like a somebody and you will be absolutely amazed at the wonderful changes that will take place.

Save yourself a lot of frustration and bring a new sense of freedom and relaxation to your relationships by practicing this universal law of mind and spirit:

> I can change no other person by direct action.
> I can change only myself. When I change,
> others tend to change in response to me.

Love Keeps No Records

You may call it hurt feelings, righteous indignation, or something else, but our love often goes out the window when another person offends us. The truth is that people do make mistakes and almost everyone will eventually do something that offends us. No human relationship can endure without a great deal of forbearance and making allowances for each other's mistakes, faults, and grievances. In the Bible we read these key words: "Bear with each other and forgive whatever grievances you may have against one another. Forgive as the Lord forgave you" (Colossians 3:13).

This story is told about John D. Rockefeller, the tycoon who built the great Standard Oil empire. It seems that Rockefeller was a man who demanded high performance from his company executives.

One day one of his executives made a $2 million mistake. Can you imagine? A $2 million mistake! News of this man's fiasco soon spread through the executive offices. During the entire day, the executives made themselves scarce and wouldn't even go near John D. Rockefeller's office, for fear of his reaction to this mistake.

Then one brave executive decided he would go ahead and keep his appointment to see Mr. Rockefeller. As the executive walked in the door, the oil monarch was writing on a piece of paper, but he looked up and abruptly said, "I guess you have heard about the $2 million mistake our friend made."

"Yes," the executive said, expecting Rockefeller to explode at any second.

Then Rockefeller said, "I've been listing all the good qualities of our friend here on a sheet of paper, and I've discovered that in the past he has made us many times more money than the amount he lost for us today by one big mistake. His good points far outweigh the one human error and I think we ought to forgive him, don't you?"

Yes, forgiveness is what it takes to really love and overlook a multitude of faults!

Learn to Love God's Way

Remember, God's kind of love is magnanimous: It looks at people in the best light. It looks for the good and overlooks the bad. Love sees the grand possibilities in another person and then proceeds to bring them out of that person.

This does not mean that love is unrealistic. Yes, it sees what's wrong with another person, but then it chooses to see all that is right. Love sees that the evil can be overcome with good and mistakes can be learning experiences.

When Jesus looks at you, He doesn't focus on your ugly spots, your sins, shortcomings, and faults. He sees you as a person of worth and value. He sees your potential. He sees what you can become with His help.

I like the words of Michelangelo when he looked at a rough chunk of cast-off marble and exclaimed, "I see an angel." Then he chiseled and carved with tender care until out of a rough, shapeless piece of marble came a beautiful angel that has inspired millions.

Love is an ever-present, beautiful possibility! God has given you love to give to others, so don't block it; don't stop it! *Whatever you do, don't let the warts stop your love.* If your love is stopped, you have no one to point the finger of blame at except yourself. No one can stop your love from flowing but you!

I love the following story:

"Do you like dollies?" the little girl asked her houseguest.

"Yes, very much," the man responded.

"Then I'll show you mine," she said. Thereupon she presented, one by one, a whole family of dolls.

"Now tell me," the visitor asked, "which is your favorite doll?"

The child hesitated for a moment and then she said, "You're quite sure you like dollies, and will you please promise not to smile if I show you my favorite?"

The man solemnly promised, and the girl hurried from the room. In a moment she returned with a tattered and dilapidated old doll. Its hair had come off; its nose was broken; its cheeks were scratched; an arm and a leg were missing. "Well, well," said the visitor, "and why do you like this one best?"

"I love her most," said the little girl, "because if I didn't love her, no one else would."

You, my friend, are chosen by God to love. There are people who desperately need your love! So, don't let the warts stop your love. Let love flow!

Thinking About Love

1. What are some of the things you see in other people that bug you? Draw a circle and write under it the name of someone who bugs you. For every fault that person has that bothers you, put a dot in the circle. Now, how much space do the dots take when compared with all the space left in the circle? What do you learn from this demonstration?

2. "Love overlooks a multitude of faults" (*see* 1 Peter 4:8). In your own relationships, what does this mean? What happens when we expect other people to be perfect?

- employees
- our mate
- our children
- fellow church members
- our pastor

3. What happens in our relationships when we major on minors? What does the Bible have to say about nagging? (*See* Ephesians 6:4; Proverbs 17:1.)

4. "Get off the judgment seat and get on the mercy seat." What does this mean to you? What happens to love when we judge other people? What happens to love when we have mercy and understanding toward other people? Read Proverbs 10:12.

5. Pick someone you know well and write down the ways in which that person is different from you. Are there people excluded from your circle of love simply because they are different or have different opinions from you? What happens if we refuse to love everyone who disagrees with us or is different from us?

6. What happens to love when we are always trying to change the other person? What are we communicating to them? What can happen in the relationship if we stop trying to change the other person?

7. What does the Bible mean in 1 Corinthians 13:5 when it says, "[Love] . . . keeps no record of wrongs"? Also read Colossians 3:13. When it comes to overlooking faults and loving people in spite of their warts, what does God teach us by word and example in Romans 5:8?

8
Speaking the Truth in Love

Some years ago I was counseling a beautiful couple. I could hardly believe it when I learned they were on the verge of divorce, because from outward appearances, their marriage seemed blissful. They didn't fight or yell at each other; there was no abuse or unfaithfulness. Outwardly, they were cordial, even kind and considerate of each other. What, then, had created the gulf between them? As we talked, it came out that both of them had made it a habit to be accommodating, without ever expressing their own true feelings.

The young man, brought up in a home with an overbearing, verbally abusive father, had made up his mind that the last thing in the world he wanted to do was be like his father. When he married, instead of expressing any negative feelings about his wife's wants or demands, he suppressed them and made a habit of accommodating her. All the time he thought he was being so nice, he was storing up unresolved anger. After years of denying his true emotions, he said as he sat in my office, "I do not love her." He hated himself for not living up to the biblical standard that says, "Husbands, love your wives" (Ephesians 5:25). His Christian faith didn't match with what he really felt about his wife and marriage.

What a joy it was to teach him the principle I am going to share with you now. This principle became the solution to my friend's problem. In fact, when I met him years later, he was still happily married and very much in love with his wife.

The deepest, most satisfying relationships between people are built on a principle I call "Truthing it in Love."

Speak the Truth in Love

Speaking the truth in love is Christ's better way for us to live and relate. Jesus said, "I am the way and the truth and the life" (John 14:6). Jesus came into a world of sham, pretense, and deception, bringing truth and change. The Christian life is to be one of walking in the light and applying the truth of Jesus to our everyday lives.

Christ's way stands in direct contrast and opposition to the way of Satan, who is the author of deception and lies. You see, deception is not new; it is ancient history. Jeremiah the prophet said, thousands of years ago, "The heart is deceitful above all things and beyond cure. Who can understand it?" (Jeremiah 17:9). The pages of every history book are filled with men's lies and deceptions.

Dishonesty is a hard road to travel: all its results are

undesirable. One lie leads to many others and destroys self-respect. Sooner or later, a lie will always come back to haunt and trouble the liar. Lying and deception destroy trust in a relationship—damage that cannot be easily repaired.

Do you like to be lied to? No!

Do you like to be deceived? No!

Do you like to be given only half the truth? No!

Do you appreciate being the victim of deception? No!

Then what makes you think that anyone else would like you for lying to them?

The fact that our society is shot through with dishonesty is no excuse for personal dishonesty. Jesus has a better way for us to live. As disciples of Jesus, we are to become brand-new and different people. This is what the Scripture says to us: "Stop lying to each other; tell the truth, for we are parts of each other and when we lie to each other we are hurting ourselves" (Ephesians 4:25 TLB).

Speaking the truth in love is the only way to enjoy lasting relationships. There are no meaningful, enduring relationships without speaking the truth to each other in love. This means that we have to learn to communicate the truth in our relationships and become open enough to receive it from other people.

Speaking the truth in love beats being two-faced. Learning to confront another person honestly is far superior to becoming a grumbling, backbiting critic. The Bible admonishes us to "Do everything without complaining or arguing" (Philippians 2:14). Moses warned the grumbling children of Israel, "You are not grumbling against us, but against the Lord" (Exodus 16:8). It is so easy to become a negative, murmuring grumbler! It's also easy to slip into talking about someone to another person instead of talking directly to the person with whom you are upset. But talking about another person behind his back certainly doesn't make for good relationships.

Learning to speak the truth in love is good mental health. One thing about being open and truthful is that you do not have to worry and fret, trying to remember what you told someone. When you tell the truth, the story is always the same. This relieves you of some tension and keeps all that tension from building up inside. When you stuff things inside instead of facing them and taking care of them, what you are really doing is making yourself sick.

Jesus has a better way for us to live. He said, "Then you will know the truth, and the truth will set you free" (John 8:32). Later in the same passage, He added, "So if the Son sets you free, you will be free indeed" (v. 36). The way to be spiritually free is to let Jesus teach you how to know and speak the truth in love.

Speaking the truth in love is one of the ways we grow as persons. Prizing truth also helps us grow in our spiritual walk with Jesus. It is one of the ways that we become more like Christ. Deception and lying certainly aren't like Jesus. You know who deceives and lies. Who wants to be like the devil? The more we walk with the Lord in the light of the truth about Him and ourselves, the more we are going to grow. When a relationship operates on this principle of speaking the truth in love, both people and the relationship grow. This fulfills God's purpose that we be growing persons, and it glorifies God.

How to Speak the Truth in Love

Get in touch with your feelings and learn to communicate those feelings in a nonthreatening way to others. It's okay to have feelings; we all have them. We have positive feelings of love, joy, and goodwill toward others, and we have negative feelings of fear, anxiety, and inadequacy. It's okay to have some negative feelings from time to time—they're a natural part of life.

However, the way we handle our negative feelings becomes one of the key factors in determining whether we are going to have a happy or miserable life. When you have negative feelings, don't deny them or suppress them. Learn to identify them and deal with them. Before you can speak the truth in love, you've got to get in touch with your own feelings.

Let me illustrate: While we were planning our three-thousand-seat sanctuary, I got very upset at the architect and said some things that strained our relationship. Later I felt guilty and knew I needed to apologize and get it straightened out.

At first I didn't know why I had acted in such a rude way. When I traced the cause of my feelings, I discovered that I thought I had told the architect about something I wanted in the plans. In fact, I thought I had told him on three or four occasions. Now, as he presented me with the final plans, what I had requested was not in them.

Once I traced the cause of my anger, I apologized for not being kind to the architect. Then I was able to proceed in an atmosphere of goodwill and point out that I had requested these things in the original plan and still wanted them. The architect responded positively and took care of the problem. Truth in love won the day! The next time you have negative feelings toward someone, trace the cause and have the honesty to report your feelings to the other person.

You do have to be careful how you report your feelings, which brings us to the next point: Learn how to confront issues and problems without attacking the person. You must share your feelings with others in ways that do not put them down or put them on the defensive. You do this by speaking of your own feelings and shortcomings, not theirs. Avoid *you* messages. Talk about what you feel, not what the other person has or has not done.

Imagine a wife criticizing her husband as he sits at the dinner table and hides behind his newspaper. She says, "I wish you wouldn't slurp your coffee," with the expected negative results. What did she really mean to say? What she really wanted to communicate was something like this: "I feel hurt when you hide behind the newspaper instead of talking to me." Unfortunately, her true feelings never got expressed, because she communicated no true feelings. Instead, she picked a fight. Picking at another person is not communicating love.

Be honest with God about what is right and what is wrong, then ask for help and guidance in your daily life. The Holy Spirit, who has been sent by Father God to live with us, is a wonderful teacher, *if* we will let Him teach us. Because God loves us just as we are, we can be open with Him about what's right and wrong in our lives, about our strengths and our weaknesses. The Holy Spirit is with us, teaching us how to overcome weaknesses and turn them into strengths. He will also teach us how to understand the various people with whom we relate, and how to be sensitive to what's going on in their lives.

In another chapter, I related how Carolyn Koons was seriously damaged as a child when she believed exaggerations and untruths about herself. Most of us have done the same thing in some area of our lives. Since we believe exaggerations and untruths about ourselves, we also tend to believe them about others. How do we change our thinking about someone else? By being honest and open with God and letting Him teach us how to relate with others in an understanding spirit.

When Should You Speak the Truth?

God's goal for our lives and relationships is understanding, not misunderstanding. John 21 describes a time when Jesus confronted Simon Peter about his failure in love and his fickleness. In this passage, we see Jesus loving Peter. He was sensitive to Peter's ability to receive the truth and brought him to a point of responsibility and recommitment.

Three times Jesus asked a penetrating question of Peter, who had denied Him: "Do you love me?" As difficult as it was to do, Jesus had to face Peter and ask him this question—not once, not twice, but three times. It was for Peter's sake that Jesus asked the question. Because of Jesus' loving confrontation, Peter found forgiveness of sin and freedom from his guilt. His relationship with Jesus was completely restored.

We learn three things from Jesus in this confrontation. First, to speak the truth in love, we must have love for the other person. Second, we must be sensitive to the other person's ability to receive the truth. Third, we must be willing to continue the relationship as the other person works out his problem.

I remember a situation in which a person I cared a great deal for was being hurt by another. My first reaction was to come to the rescue of the one I cared about, to call the other person up and give him a piece of my mind. I don't like to see people I love being hurt.

When your emotions have heated up, it's best to wait until you cool down before you do any confronting. I didn't follow this rule. I picked the telephone up and dialed the number, ready to let the person have it. Fortunately, he wasn't home. Having to wait to talk to him caused me to spend time in prayer. As I prayed, a sound mind and love returned to me. Later in the day, I was able to reach the person and, out of a heart of love, speak the truth in a way he could receive it. The problem was corrected, and the relationships restored.

There are four times when you should definitely speak the truth in love.

When You Are Going to Blow Up if You Don't Open Up

How many times have you had someone irritate you and you said, "I don't want to make waves"? So you stored a stick of dynamite inside yourself. Then the next thing happened, and you stored another stick. And another stick. We all have a level at which we can't tolerate any more sticks, then some little thing happens, the fuse is lit, and *boom!*

The way to avoid emotional blowups is to open up and talk about the daily things that irritate you—when they happen. Take care of the daily irritations and you'll avoid the big blowup.

When Another Person Is Hurting You

Is it fair to build resentment against another person for something he is doing or not doing when he is unaware of what is happening? In every relationship there comes a time when the air needs to be cleared. The thing I appreciate about my wife, Margi, is that if something bothers her, it's not long until she tells me. I don't have to try to guess what I've done or haven't done that might be bothering her. She reports honestly and openly on her feelings, and then I can deal with them. If I need to correct something, I do.

> **Open sharing about both good and bad
> things makes for healthy, happy
> relationships.**

You might ask the person who has hurt you, "Did you mean to hurt me?" Nine out of ten times, people don't mean to hurt others. Most of the time, they don't even know they've hurt you. So report honestly on your feelings in a nonattacking way. Get it out in the open and talk about it.

> **"Speak truth in love." What beautiful words!
> They really do make a difference in a
> relationship.**

When Other People Are Being Hurt by What Is Going On

At our church growth conference, a pastor who had been at the same church for many years shared with me how deeply hurt he was. It seemed that last summer, while he was taking a vacation, the wife of one of his associates went from person to person saying untrue things about him. People he had counted as his friends for years just let her do it. In three weeks, she almost destroyed a pastor and the relationships he had built over fifteen years—because good people kept silent.

> **The strength of a church is unity. Together, we achieve great things for God. Divided, we become powerless in a world of conflict.**

One of the keys to maintaining unity in a church (or any group) is for mature people to nip destructive criticism in the bud by speaking the truth in love to those who are disturbing the peace.

When There Is Love in Your Heart

Never confront a difficult subject or issue with another person until there is love in your heart. Without love, the truth is like a sledgehammer coming down on top of a person: it can do nothing but damage. The truth is to be spoken through tears of love that heal, build up a person, and make him better.

The first thing you must do before you speak the truth in love is spend time praying for the other person. While you are praying, be sure to check your own motives and see that they are right. Your purpose must be constructive, not destructive. Remember, love is never hard or harsh, crude or rude. If you really love someone, what you want is the best for him.

When speaking the truth in love, watch your timing. Is the person tired? Not a good time! Does the person have other heavy problems right now? Not a good time! Just before eating, or at the dinner table? Not a good time! In front of other people who have nothing to do with it? Not a good time! Be sensitive to the other person and find the best time to approach him or her. On the other hand, don't keep putting off what you need to do as soon as possible.

We've seen that there are things that can be done when love goes wrong. You *can* repair a damaged relationship. By avoiding Spoiler Attitudes, not expecting perfection from yourself or others, choosing to act and speak the truth in love, you can strengthen the relationships you cherish and learn to love with Jesus' kind of love—a love that never fails.

Thinking About Love

1. Describe what speaking the truth without love is like. Describe what speaking the truth with love is like. Evaluate yourself on a scale from 1 to 10 as to how effectively you think you are doing this.

2. What happens when we hold things inside, telling ourselves that we don't want to make waves?

3. List at least four reasons we need to learn to speak the truth in love. What does Ephesians 4:15 identify as the goal of speaking the truth in love?

4. How does a person learn to get in touch with feelings and communicate those feelings to others in a nonthreatening way? What's wrong with sending *you* messages? Think about the last time you confronted someone, and ask yourself whether you communicated love or something else.

5. How well do you receive truths spoken in love from another person?

6. How can we get love in our hearts before confronting another person?

9
You Can Win
With Love

Two boys are on a teeter-totter, having a wonderful time. Suddenly one gets the idea to have a little fun at the expense of his playmate. The moment his end is down, he jumps off the teeter-totter, bringing the other boy down with an unexpected crash. Having been taken advantage of and not wanting to get hurt again, the other boy refuses to play anymore.

But the boy is very persuasive, and he finally gets his little friend to play again. This time the other boy jumps off the teeter-totter when his end is down, and the first is brought crashing with a thud to the ground.

Now neither boy will trust the other, so they cannot play together anymore. First one broke the law of love, then the other broke it. As a result, each boy lost the friendship of the other. Who won? Who lost? They both lost.

Without love, we all lose.

Without love, our relationships neither do well nor last. When you stop and think about it, you know that from your own experience. Without love, we quickly rub each other the wrong way. Conflict and misunderstanding replace communication and understanding. Relationships are torn apart.

Love is the winningest thing there is in the world! I have seen it:

- mend broken relationships
- rebuild broken lives
- change an uncontrollable brat into a likeable child
- transform a rebellious teenager into a responsible person
- build bridges across impossible chasms

First Corinthians 13 says it all:

Love is very patient and kind, never jealous or envious, never boastful or proud, never haughty or selfish or rude. Love does not demand its own way. It is not irritable or touchy. It does not hold grudges and will hardly even notice when others do it wrong. It is never glad about injustice, but rejoices whenever truth wins out. If you love someone you will be loyal to him no matter what the cost. You will always believe in him, always expect the best of him, and always stand your ground in defending him.

1 Corinthians 13:4–7 TLB

> **No matter what happens to you, love is always your greatest possibility.**

Selfish People Lose!

The Bible is a book full of drama. Its stories are of real people and the happenings in their lives. In one very dramatic scene in the third chapter of 1 Kings, we see two mothers claiming the same baby. Not being able to settle the dispute any other way, they took the baby to King Solomon and asked him to decide.

This was before the days of blood tests, so the king had no real way of knowing who was the baby's mother. Solomon asked that a sword be brought to him, then raised the sword as if to cut the baby in two and give half to each woman. Here we see vividly the futility of the sword. The sword brings only death. It never, never brings people together.

If the king had used the sword and cut the baby in half, he would have accomplished nothing but destruction. He would have robbed the world of a life. Whenever we choose to fight another person with a sword, nothing is accomplished except destruction and the robbing of joyful, abundant living.

The real mother cried out in love that the other woman could have the baby, rather than see it cut in half. Her love for the child won out over her own urgent desire to have her child. She loved her child so much that she was willing to lose him in order to save him.

Solomon in his wisdom immediately saw who was the true, loving mother and gave the child to her.

> **Love wins by giving up selfishness.**

The Bible teaches us, "Love does not demand its own way" (1 Corinthians 13:5 TLB). Whenever we demand our own way no matter how much it hurts other people, we are being selfish. Selfishness never finds love; it destroys love. Selfishness never brings people together; it always separates them. The selfish person always ends up isolated and alone. The more selfish you are, the more you are going to lose love. As Leo Buscaglia said in *Love*, "Love is always open arms. If you close your arms about love, you will find that you are left holding only yourself."

Jesus Came to Love Losers Into Winners

Right now, I want you to use your imagination. The place is heaven. Like the coach talking to his quarterback in the last seconds before the final play, Father God is talking to the Son, Jesus. What do you think He is saying? What was the last word God gave to Jesus before sending Him on His important mission to earth?

What God said to Jesus was so life-changing! So overpowering! So motivating! So beautiful!

What departing message did God give to Jesus to

bring to us? God said to His Son, Jesus, "Give them all My love!"

The Living Bible says it this way: "When we were utterly helpless with no way of escape, Christ came at just the right time and died for us sinners who had no use for him" (Romans 5:6).

There is no greater love than this: "While we were yet sinners, Christ died for us" (v. 8).

Jesus Loved Without Discrimination

Jesus' own people turned against Him because He ate with sinners. At Jacob's well, He encountered an adulterous woman from the hated Samaritan race, but instead of snubbing her and treating her like dirt, He saw her potential and value and helped her to become a child of God. Jesus loves sinners like you and me.

Jesus Loves in Spite of Unloveliness

Jesus does not withhold His love—He gives it! He does not say, "Reform, do as I say, and *then* I will love you." He loves us first. Jesus loves us as we are, with our strengths and weaknesses, our pasts and our futures. Even after they had spit in His face as He died on the cross for our sins, He said, "Father, forgive them, for they do not know what they are doing " (Luke 23:34). Isn't the love of Jesus something wonderful?

Because Jesus comes to you, giving you all of God's love, you have a big decision to make. You may either accept His love and be changed by it or reject it and go on in your selfish, self-destructive way without God's love. This is something you must accept or reject for yourself. God tries every way possible to win you to Himself, but if you persistently say no, He will respect your decision and let you have your own way. No one can make this decision for you. You cannot escape this decision. You cannot cop out. You are responsible throughout all eternity for the decision you make.

How do you receive Jesus? By asking Him to come into your life and by becoming His disciple. To be Jesus' disciple means that you follow Him and His teachings and learn how to live His way.

Being a Christian is a lifetime of learning how to put God's love into practice.

God's love goes beyond the limits of any definition we can give it. It does things that are humanly impossible. It enables you to love people who, in your own strength, you could never love.

You just can't stop love.

- It breaks through thick barriers.
- It climbs over insurmountable walls.
- It builds bridges across chasms.

You can win with love.

- It overlooks faults.
- It forgives and forgets.
- It brings us back together.

You can win with love.

- It tunes in.
- It understands.
- It gives.

You can win with love.

- It goes the extra mile.
- It works hard.
- It never gives up.

You can win with love!

- Because the Bible says God's kind of love never fails.

Before Love Can Flow, You've Got to Let Go!

Many times we stop the flow of God's love in our lives because we hold on to things and emotions that we need to let go. Our holding on acts like a dam that stops the natural flow of God's love through our lives. The moment we become God's children, we are born of love; He places His great supernatural love in our hearts. From that moment on, it is His will that love flow through our lives and relationships like a mighty river.

In fact, in Romans 5:5 we read about this great treasure of love that is ours as God's children: "God has poured out his love into our hearts by the Holy Spirit, whom he has given us." In the context, God has been talking about demonstrating His love for us while we were yet sinners. This great unconditional, unstoppable love is not only to be received by us but is to flow through our lives to others.

Is it flowing through your life? Is it flowing into your relationships? Is His love healing you? Is it lifting you? If so, praise the Lord. If not, why not? You are holding on to something you need to let go. For this river of love to flow through your life, you have to let go. Let go of anything that stops the flow of God's love through your life.

Let go! Let go!

- Let go of fear.
- Let go of rights.
- Let go of vengeance.
- Let go of the past.
- Let go of things.
- Let go of blame.
- Let go of your smashed pride.
- Let go of grievances.

Jesus sent the Holy Spirit to be our cleanser. Along the road of life we get dusty and dirty, and we need cleansing of the spirit. Before we can be filled with the Spirit, we must be cleansed by the Spirit from our self-seeking and self-serving, in any or all areas of rebellion in our lives.

The Holy Spirit wants to give you a new, clean heart and to renew your attitude. To refresh your spirit. To forgive you from all sin and unrighteousness.

From the year 1974 to 1979, Julian Carroll served as the distinguished governor of Kentucky. In some of the political maneuvering that took place, the governor was the victim of an all-out attack against his reputation. Unsubstantiated accusations appeared daily in the press, and all kinds of unjust things were said against him.

By Carroll's own testimony, bitterness crept into his spirit, his wife's, and his children's. They even stopped going to church.

Then one day the governor was invited to a luncheon of Christian businessmen. There the Holy Spirit touched him in a new way and began to show him that his bitterness was wrong. The governor confessed it and the Holy Spirit came that day and cleansed him and freed him of the bondage of resentment.

You see, when the Spirit is given freedom to work within us, there is great liberty. The devil is the one who wants to get us all bound up in the old feelings.

With this new indwelling and infilling of the Holy Spirit, the governor was able to flow with the Spirit and forgive those who had injured him.

We can never experience real joy in our lives until we have the power of the Holy Spirit to forgive.

Forgiveness Is the Cure

Because you are a human being with feelings, living among other human beings who have imperfections, you are going to get wounded emotionally from time to time. Without the saving grace of forgiveness, this wound will make you sick. Without forgiveness, there is no inner healing. Without forgiveness, there are no enduring relationships in our lives.

Jesus came to give us forgiveness and teach us how to forgive one another. When we forgive Christ's way, we become healthy. When we refuse to forgive, we become sick on the inside. Unfortunately, there are a lot of sick people in our society today.

Jesus said, "Your heavenly Father will forgive you if you forgive those who sin against you; but if *you* refuse to forgive *them, he* will not forgive *you*" (Matthew 6:14, 15 TLB). What does this mean? It means that when you stop forgiving others, you block the flow of God's love and forgiveness into your own life. As followers of Jesus, we are to follow His example and be the first to forgive. If anyone has done something wrong to you or to a member of your family, whether or not that person ever asks you to forgive him, for your own health and well-being, you must forgive him.

If you have a strained relationship with another person, the sooner you take responsibility for your part in causing the breakdown in the relationship, the better. Go to the person and speak these three healing words: *I am sorry.* For the best results when asking for forgiveness, follow these rules:

- The sooner you ask for forgiveness, the better.
- Confess no one's sins but your own.
- After stating what you've done wrong, say you are sorry and ask, "Will you forgive me, please?"

Here's a story that shows the power of forgiveness:

For thirty minutes, Martha went on a nonstop tirade describing every one of her husband's faults and mistakes over the years. Her pastor listened attentively. When she finally ran down, he looked her in the eye and gently said, "Martha, have you ever forgiven your husband for all his many faults and mistakes?" Then he added, "There are no enduring marriages without a lot of forgiveness."

Martha became angry because the pastor had not agreed that her husband was a bum. Not hearing what she had wanted to hear, she got up to leave. With great compassion, the pastor said to her, "Martha, would you think about what I've said to you? I've said it to you because it's the truth. I love you and your husband, Ted. And I want God's best for you."

At home that week, Martha began to do some very serious thinking about what the pastor had said. One night when she couldn't sleep, she began to open up and pray to God about how she felt. Soon the Spirit of God began to show her the ugly garbage that had built up in her because of her unforgiving spirit. As she reflected in the mirror of her soul, she didn't like the person she had become.

The next week she went back to the pastor and began to talk about what was wrong with her. The pastor helped her to see that she was responsible for the sick spirit inside of her. Because she had not forgiven her husband over the years, these things had mounted up and become a brick wall damaging their relationship. Her own unwillingness to forgive had actually separated her from the love of her husband.

That morning, in the quietness of the pastor's study, she surrendered herself and her ill feelings to Christ. She rededicated her life to Jesus and got herself straightened out with her Master. She owned up to her need for revenge, confessed it as sin, and asked God to forgive her. Martha asked God to give her forgiveness for her husband, to teach her how to love him unconditionally.

A couple of weeks later Ted, who in the past wouldn't even go to church with his wife, went to see the pastor. He couldn't believe the change that had taken place in his wife and in their marriage. Martha's change had made him realize what an indifferent husband he had become. Ted confessed his own sins, selfishness, and need for Christ. That day he became a brand-new person in Christ Jesus, went home to ask his wife for forgiveness, and began to put God's kind of love into practice in their home.

Isn't the forgiveness and love of Jesus something wonderful?

With Love You Win

It's not always easy to love. Was it easy for Jesus when they spit in His face? Was it easy for Jesus when they ridiculed Him? Is it easy to love someone who despises you? Is it easy to love when someone acts in a hateful, vengeful way toward you? Is it easy to love when your whole world is turned upside down?

Jesus didn't promise us that it would be easy to love, but He did say, "By this all men will know that you are my disciples, if you love one another" (John 13:35).

My friend, when in the Name of Jesus you keep putting love into practice, somehow, some way, you are going to be a winner.

> **With love, you always win. Not once, not twice, but again and again.**

Somehow, someway, love always finds a way to come through and win.

Dr. Norman Vincent Peale's wife, Ruth, tells this true story in her book *The Adventures of Being a Wife:*

> Jack Kyle was Chief Engineer of the New York Authority. . . . He and his wife were about as close as it is possible for a couple to be. Virginia was a gentle, very beautiful, highly intelligent woman. It was a terrible blow to all of us when she was stricken with cancer. The doctors said that nothing could be done; that it was just a matter of time. . . .
>
> In the hospital, Virginia's condition steadily worsened. Her husband spent hours at her bedside. Then suddenly, with no warning, a heart attack struck Jack.

He lingered a few days. Then came a second attack and he was dead.

It was impossible to keep the truth from his wife, when her husband did not come to see her. She guessed—and no one had the heart to hide the sad fact from her. She asked quietly when the funeral was to be. When told that it was to be Sunday at the Marble Collegiate Church, at two-thirty, she said that she was going to be there. In her condition the doctor said that was impossible. But she would not accept this. She kept saying that she was going to be there.

One-half hour before the funeral, Virginia Kyle died. And when Norman conducted the service for her husband, no one in the church had any doubts. Virginia had said she would be there. And she was.

> **With Christ's love you somehow always win!**

Thinking About Love

1. Why is love the winningest thing in all the world?

2. What effect does selfishness have on love?

3. Describe the kind of love God gives us (Romans 5:8). How does this differ from the kind of love we see in our world today?

4. What does a person have to do to get God's love flowing in and through his or her life?

5. List things you need to let go of in order for love to flow through your life.

6. How did Jesus say the world would know we were His disciples? (*See* John 13:35.)

10
How to Love a Woman

How do you love a woman? Ephesians 5:25–33 teaches us that a man should love a woman the same way that Jesus loved and gave Himself for the church. It also teaches us to give the same tender loving care to our wives that we give to our own bodies. Loving your wife means discovering her basic needs and doing what you can do to meet them. Everyone has the need to love and be loved and to feel worthwhile. Anytime you do what you can to make your wife feel loved and worthwhile, you are performing an act of love.

The Scriptures teach us that to be a disciple of Jesus means to follow Him and to learn how to love others His way. As Christian men, we are to follow Jesus and learn how to love our wives. We must make this the number-one priority in our lives.

Twelve Ways to Love a Woman

Vote Her Number One

The number-one need in a wife's life is her husband's attention. It was your attention that won her for you in the first place. Without attention, love dies. Without attention, marriage dies. Without attention, friendship dies. Without attention, no relationship will survive, much less thrive and grow.

I once heard about a man who loved to watch football games so much that he would come home on Friday night, start watching football, and be glued to the television the entire weekend. One weekend his wife hadn't heard a sound out of him at all and was a little worried about whether he was still alive. Then she walked into the front room and heard him belch, so she knew he was at least breathing.

By Sunday night she had had it. Angrily she strode into the room, turned the television off, then broke into tears and said, "You don't love me!" Before he could reply, she said, "You love football more than you love me."

He replied, "But I love you more than basketball."

A woman needs to know that she is number one in her husband's life and that she comes before job, before church, and before sports. She has to know she is the apple of his eye.

Verify Her Feelings

We had been married only a couple of years when Margi went to the grocery store and discovered at the checkout line that she didn't have enough money. She was embarrassed, and when she came home, she was in tears. I asked her what was wrong, and she started to cry all the more. When I finally began to get the story out of her, my first impulse was to laugh. To me it was funny, and I wondered what the big deal was. But when I saw the hurt in her eyes, I did something smart: I kept my mouth shut, walked over, put my arms around her, and held her.

I have to confess, it took me years to understand that Margi wanted understanding from me, not solutions. You know, preachers are very adept at giving little sermons—it's what God called us to do—so in my everyday world, I am always solving problems. If this is the problem, then that is the solution. That's exactly the type of logic that gets men in trouble with their wives!

I cannot overemphasize this point: *Women need to have their feelings validated and accepted.* It's not solutions they seek, but understanding. Listen. Hold them. Let them know it's okay to feel as they do. Then maybe a little later on they will be ready to accept a suggestion. A woman will love a man who validates her feelings.

Share Yourself With Her

Your wife wants to know what's going on in your world. What have you been doing all day? If you don't share your world with her, she is going to feel left out and rejected. Being friends means sharing each other's world.

One of the ways men and women are different is that a man's way of feeling close is to say, "Let's have sex." The woman says, "Let's talk." She wants her man to be interested in her world. If he shows no interest and won't listen, then she takes that as a personal affront and feels rejected. And when she is rejected, she doesn't feel like responding.

Listen to Her

You can meet many of your wife's needs if you will just listen. The first thing that goes into creating a love relationship is listening. Admittedly it is much harder to listen than to talk. I have found that it is harder to listen intensely than it is to talk to thousands of people.

Lovers listen to each other. Unfortunately, the average American husband and wife talk to each other for about eleven minutes a day, and most of that conversation is on the surface. When you are in love, you listen. I'm not talking about half-listening, with your mind somewhere else. I mean listening not only to what she says but what she *means*. Try to understand what she's feeling underneath her words. Believe me! If you really listen to her, your wife will love you.

Wrap Her Packages

The first Christmas Margi and I were married, we lived in our little honeymoon house. Weeks ahead of Christmas we started decorating the house. I did lots of shopping to buy just the right gifts for her, but because I didn't know a few things about women, I made a big mistake: I hurriedly wrapped the packages in a haphaz-ard way, never realizing that the wrapping was impor-tant. When Margi saw the Christmas packages I had for her, she cried! All those special gifts I had bought for her, and there she was crying. I didn't understand what was going on.

I discovered that day that how a package is wrapped is important, too. That kind of stuff really means some-thing. It doesn't mean much to *me*; I just want to get to the gift and hold it in my hand, but I'm not Margi. Do those special things that add beauty and luster to your continuing courtship.

Express Love to Her

Your wife wants to be shown by word and action that you love her. If you love her, tell her so. Do you want a more exciting marriage? Then never stop courting and finding ways to express your love.

The disciple John, who, with the maturing of years abounded with love, said it this way: "Dear friends, let us practice loving each other, for love comes from God and those who are loving and kind show that they are the children of God, and that they are getting to know him better" (1 John 4:7 TLB).

One evening when I had to be away from home, I stopped at a phone booth and called Margi, my wife. I said, "I called to tell you I love you, and I think you are the neatest." I noticed that several days later, she was still talking about this. Then a few days later, Margi surprised me by going and buying me some clothes she thought I needed. I liked the clothes, but better yet, I felt loved. Do you want your marriage to be exciting? Then never, never stop expressing your love.

Christ's kind of love will carry you through almost every storm of life. The only way this kind of love can come in and stay in your heart is for the Spirit of Christ to come into your life. Somehow the self-centered backbone in our spirit has to be broken. This is what Christians mean by "conversion" or being "born again." Christ comes in and changes the basic attitude. The most important thing in any marriage is having Jesus Christ.

How our homes need Christ's saving love, which is "never haughty or selfish or rude. Love does not demand its own way. It is not irritable or touchy. It does not hold grudges and will hardly even notice when others do it wrong" (1 Corinthians 13:5 TLB). What a love Jesus gives!

Many a man has said, "I am not affectionate. That's not my nature." My response to that is, "That's a cop-out. Your wife needs affection, and any person alive can learn to be affectionate. With God's help, you can open up and change."

Here are some tips on becoming a more affectionate husband:

- Hug and kiss your wife every morning while you're still in bed.
- Tell her you love her.
- Kiss her before you leave for work.

- Call her during the day to see how she is doing.
- Remember special occasions (birthday, anniversary, Valentine's Day, Mother's Day). Learn how to shop for a woman.
- When you arrive home from work, give her a hug and kiss and spend a few minutes talking to her about her day.
- Help with dishes after dinner.
- Hug and kiss her every night before you go to sleep.

Remember this, men: Sex begins with affection. Affection is the environment of the marriage; sex is the event.

Edify Her as a Person

How do you edify (build up) a woman? By paying attention to little things and letting her know you appreciate her and she is of value to you. A husband can painfully wound his wife by failure to comment on a meal that she has carefully prepared or by not noticing and appreciating all the little things she does to make his life more enjoyable.

Tony Campolo tells about being with a married couple when a young woman walked by in her bikini. Tony's friend said out loud, "Hey, Tony, look at that! Isn't she really something?" Tony said he wanted to punch the guy out. There sat the guy's wife, withering and feeling ugly in comparison.

To love your wife as your own body means to adore her, to build her up, to let her know how much you really value her. One of the best things you can do for yourself and your wife is to make her feel special!

Encourage Her to Develop and Become

Your wife is a person with very special talents, gifts, and abilities. If you encourage her to develop and become, she will bloom like a flower in beauty. If you hold her back, squelch her, dominate her, she will wither, and when she withers, she will hate you for it.

Love frees. Love encourages. Love allows the other person to become herself. Accept the fact that your wife is different from you—beautifully, wonderfully different. Do you understand the difference between manipulation, which is wrong, and motivation, which is right? Manipulation is trying to get someone to do what you want them to do without any regard for whether or not it is good for them. Motivation is helping someone do something good for them—something they *want* to do. The wise man motivates his wife to become everything she can be to the glory of God. Stop trying to dominate her; set her free to bloom. Then your wife will become even more beautiful to you in the passing years.

Touch Her

A woman needs nonsexual touching: a hug, holding. Touching communicates that you care. If you really care for her as a person, touching not only sends her the message that she is valuable to you but also makes her feel warm and comfortable. How will your wife know that you love her unless you touch her and hold her? Someone has said that a picture is worth a thousand words. Well, a gentle, nonsexual, loving touch is worth more than a thousand words.

Surround Her With Security and Stability

One of the greatest needs a woman has is to feel that her home is secure. She is by nature a nesting person. When the husband neglects the home, the woman feels that she is being rejected. For example, if you let that faucet go on leaking, your wife will feel that she's being neglected. She identifies with her home.

Most women these days work not only in the home but outside the home as well. One wife confided that she comes home from a hard day's work and is expected to fix dinner, do the dishes, the washing, and the housework while her husband sits on the sofa. This makes her feel pretty insecure about their relationship. A good way to make your wife feel secure is to share the duties of running a home. Besides, the more you do together, the more you are going to be together. The quicker you get the housework done together, the more free time you have to enjoy each other.

Be Her Spiritual Leader

My twenty-six years in pastoral ministry have shown me clearly that a woman wants a spiritual leader— someone she can look up to and trust, someone she can confide in, someone who will be honest and live by the rules and principles that come from a higher authority. Without this, her security is threatened.

Ephesians 5 teaches us that a man's highest calling in marriage is to be a spiritual leader, a leader who makes decisions not out of selfishness but for the good of the family. Like Christ, he serves the family in love.

Be on Her Side

Your wife needs to feel that you are always on her side. When an overwhelming problem comes up, it should not be *you and* I that deal with it, but *we*. In Genesis we learn that from one, God made two—male and female. Then in Genesis 2:24, 25, we learn that the two are to become one. *We*, together with God's help, can get through this problem.

In my book *We Are Making Our Home a Happy Place*, I told this story: A young mother left her small child unattended while she was doing the laundry in the basement. The child found some adult medicine, drank it all, and was dead upon arrival at the hospital. The mother sat, stunned and stricken, waiting for her husband to come. What would he say? He adored the child. When he did come, he took his wife in his arms and said just four words, over and over: "Darling, I love you." Nothing else—no questions, no incriminations, no blame. Just: "Darling, I love you." He forgot about his own hurt and pain and did his best to draw the protective cloak of love around his suffering wife. Now, that man had learned how to love a woman!

Thinking About Love

1. In what ways are men and women different? How does knowing or not knowing these differences affect a marriage relationship?

2. Which do you think makes for the best marriage, competition or cooperation? Why do you say so?

3. Discuss this: You can give without loving, but you cannot love without giving.

4. Take the following self-examination. If you are a married man, score yourself on how well you think you do in loving your wife. If you are a married woman, score each one on how important is to you. Use the scale 1–10, with 1 as the lowest and 10 as the highest.

_____ vote her number one
_____ verify her feelings
_____ share yourself with her
_____ listen to her
_____ wrap her packages
_____ verbally express love to her
_____ edify her as a person
_____ encourage her to develop and become
_____ touch her
_____ surround her with security and stability
_____ be the spiritual leader she can trust and confide in
_____ be on her side

11
How to Love a Man

Rather than presuming to explain to women how they should love their husbands, I have asked Margi to write this chapter. What follows is her counsel, and I think she says it well.

Last Sunday, as our family was driving to lunch after the service, we noticed a bumper sticker on the car in front of us. It said, "God made man and rested. God made woman and nobody's rested since."

I kind of like that, because it suggests how exciting women are. Men find them the most exciting and interesting creatures that God ever made. They can bring great joy into a man's life, or they can make him absolutely miserable. I hope that as I share what God is teaching me, women readers will learn how to be exciting wives and bring more joy into their family life.

Good Marriages Take Work

There are no perfect marriages, for the simple reason that there are no perfect people. If you are looking for a perfect marriage, good luck! You'll never find one. You are not perfect, and whoever you find is not perfect, either. Yet, God has given us the wonderful opportunity to be the best we can be and help our husbands be the best they can be.

Now don't say, "Oh, if my marriage were like the Galloways', it would really be good." We work very hard to make our marriage good. We're human, and we make mistakes. We fight. We don't speak to each other occasionally—not very often, but occasionally. We have problems, just as you do. My advice to you is to abandon any ideas of comparing your marriage to someone else's. Abandon any preconceived ideas of "what men are like" and just discover what your man is like, because we're all different.

I can honestly tell you that as Dale and I grow older together, I learn new things about him every day. It's exciting. He is a most interesting person. I thought I knew him when we were married, but I'm learning more and more about the wonderful person that God has created in my husband. I believe that God has given us a love that will last and last until eternity. I want the same for you.

In Ephesians 5, we read, "Wives, submit to your husbands" (v. 22). "The wife must respect her husband" (v. 33). These verses tell me my responsibility to my husband. I am accountable to God for the way I treat Dale. I am accountable to God for my attitude toward Dale. I am not particularly fond of the word *submit*. Submitting sounds as if you are inferior to someone, and I would just as soon be equals. I would like to change *submit* to *yield*, because I believe that is what it means—yield yourself to your husband's leadership. I have no problem at all yielding to my husband's leadership (unless, of course, he disagrees with me). But seriously, I believe the Bible calls husbands and wives to mutual submission or each yielding to the other.

To be a good wife, to have a good marriage, there are ten things I'd suggest you need to do.

Share Your Husband's Life

Enter into his world; find out who he really is; build a friendship together. When Dale and I first met, we met as friends. Then that friendship developed into a romance, and the romance developed into marriage. But first we built a comradeship together—a friendship. I wanted to get to know him. I was interested in what he was interested in. Today I am still interested in him and want to share his life. I enjoy being with him. He's my very best friend.

Sharing your husband's life will involve you in some things you don't particularly enjoy but do because you love him. Go to the basketball game with him. Go to the football game with him. Sit by him, hold hands, enjoy each other. Take the time to ask him about his work. Go visit where he works. Find out what his interests are, and then join him in those interests. If he fishes, go fishing. At least you'll be in a boat together. Learn all you can about your man. He is very complex, but he is very interesting.

Build Up Your Husband

In 1 Thessalonians 5:11 we read, "Therefore encourage one another and build each other up." That is such a vital part of a couple's relationship, and honest admiration is a great motivator for most men. Of course, some women overdo it. They are just in awe of their husbands, each thinking her husband is the most wonderful creature in the world and can do no wrong. That is not realistic! I can look at my husband, see his strengths and his weaknesses, and love him anyway. I can build his strengths and help him to see his potential.

Do not nag your husband. When you nag, you tear down. So what if he isn't as detailed on things as you are? So what if he can't always do the things you want him to do? Find out what he does well and build him up in those areas. If you don't admire and bless your husband, you are expecting perfection—something you will never get. Don't compare him with others or judge him—enjoy him.

Value His Ideas

Listen to your husband when he wants to talk. Many husbands are men of few words, and we wives have to learn to be quiet long enough to hear what our husbands have to say.

I've often wondered what would have happened if I had not valued Dale's idea to start a church. Where might we be today? At one time what is now a thriving church was just a dream. It was just something Dale had inside of him. What if I had shot down everything he said about starting this church? I shudder to think where we would be today, because God had His hand on Dale's life, and He was speaking through Dale's thoughts and dreams.

God may be speaking through your husband today, through his thoughts and his dreams. If you shoot down every idea he has, you may be squashing a wonderful beginning that God has in mind for your life, too. Some of his ideas will be crazy—maybe a lot of them—but just listen, because sometimes your husband needs to verbalize his ideas and get them out. He may wake up eventually and think they aren't good ideas, but until then, listen! I have not always been good at this, but I'm learning. I've been praying that God will keep me from immediately saying, "Oh, that's a dumb idea."

Have you ever said that to your husband? How do you think that makes him feel? It may be a dumb idea, but he doesn't need to hear it from you, does he? Encourage your husband and pray that God will take care of the dumb ideas.

Honor Him in Front of the Children

Respect your husband's leadership in the home. God made the husband the leader in the home, so don't usurp this role yourself. I am over the house, so to speak. I take care of it, I keep it up, and I see that it looks nice. But when it comes to the leadership of the *home*, Dale is our leader.

If you want your children to show respect for their dad, they have to see that you respect him. You are the children's model. You are the only one who can show them that Dad is special and the rightful head of the house. In our home, Dale and I usually work together at parenting, but he is our leader. So even if I don't always agree with the outcome, I yield to his authority out of respect and love for him as the leader of our home. That doesn't mean I don't give my opinion. I do! But after I give my opinion, I have to be willing to let it go.

At home, we sometimes call Dale the "sugar daddy." Sometimes dads are like that. The moms have to be the meanies, and the dads get to be the nice guys. If the kids want something, they go to Dad. They don't go to Mom, because she's tough. In your house it may just be the opposite. However it is, you have to work and learn together as a family.

Sometimes Dale makes a decision or lets the kids do something I wouldn't. Still, I respect him. I am glad that sometimes he lets the children do things I wouldn't, because I believe that brings balance into our home. Talk over the big decisions concerning the children by yourselves before you make the decision. If you don't, the kids will push one of you one way and the other another way. It's easy to be divided, and every child knows how to play one end against the other!

Be Loyal to Him

Support your husband's decisions. Learn to trust him. He loves you. Be in his corner and on his side. Loyalty is a very important ingredient in a marriage.

When Dale and I were first married, the Lord gave me a verse: "If you love someone you will be loyal to him no matter what the cost. You will always believe in him" (1 Corinthians 13:7 TLB). It doesn't just say you will believe in him but that you will *always* believe in him. "Always expect the best of him, and always stand your ground in defending him." That's loyalty! And that is what we, as women, need to be for our men.

The hardest thing for me is hearing someone talk negatively about Dale. In our kind of work, where we are up in the front and Dale is an authority, people often do criticize. It is so hard when I hear that someone doesn't like my husband. I can't imagine why. He's so special to me. But you know, that is when he needs my loyalty the most. He needs to know that I am on his side. Be on your husband's side. And when he tells you his deep thoughts or secrets, don't tell anyone else. Be loyal to him. Keep those secrets. Let him know he can trust you.

Be Responsive to His Sexual Needs

We read in 1 Corinthians 7:3, 4: "The husband should fulfill his marital duty to his wife, and likewise the wife to her husband. The wife's body does not belong to her alone but also to her husband. In the same way, the husband's body does not belong to him alone but also to his wife." The Bible says that when we become one—when we marry—we no longer have exclusive control over our own body; it is under the authority of our spouse. We have made a commitment to love our husbands sexually and to fulfill their desires.

It's not difficult to read a man's mind; it is like an open book. You need to get your mind on love and off other things. Two things are important to sexual fulfillment in your marriage. First, overcome your sexual ignorance. There are many good Christian books and many other ways to learn about sex; you don't need to be ignorant. Second, communicate your sexual understanding to each other. The best way you can learn to fulfill your husband's desires and needs is to talk to him and get him to talk to you.

Nothing will take the place of loving your husband sexually—not doing his laundry, fixing him a good dinner, providing a lovely home, or working outside the home to help with the income. These all help to please him, but the best thing you can do for him is to let yourself go and enjoy loving him sexually. God made us that way, and we need to learn how to fulfill each other in that manner.

Be a Team

Complement each other, don't compete against each other. The world is so full of competition between men and women today that it's almost sickening. God did not intend for us to compete. He intended us to complete each other, to work together. I don't want to compete with Dale. It's lonely when you're competing because you're divided and there is a gap between you. Each of us has our own strengths and weaknesses. I cover his weaknesses and he covers mine.

Two are much more than one. When he succeeds, I succeed. When he fails, I fail. I love that team spirit. Do you know why he let me write this chapter? Because we're a team and he believes in me. And I thank him for that.

Practice Forgiveness

In Colossians 3:13 we read, "Bear with each other and forgive whatever grievances you may have against one another. Forgive as the Lord forgave you." Forgiveness opens, releases, and frees. Unforgiveness closes. Unforgiveness binds.

We sometimes have a tendency to become irritated with our men and instead of communicating how we feel, we stuff it inside and let those irritations become resentments. Those resentments build into bitterness, and this can lead to the destruction of a marriage.

One of the most important elements of a marriage is practicing forgiveness. Be ready to say, "I'm sorry," even if he has not said it. Dale and I rarely go to sleep at night without practicing this principle. Many nights we have been awake until 4:00 A.M. working out our communication and forgiving each other. It takes work. It takes effort. But it is worth it! Practice forgiveness.

Pray for Your Husband

One specific area where women can get into trouble is trying to play God in the marriage. Deep down you may think you can change your husband, but no woman can draw her husband to God. The Holy Spirit does that.

I pray for my husband all the time. I feel that praying for my man is a privilege that God has given me. I know that he needs my prayers, and when I pray for him, it is so much easier to accept him for who he is. You see, I don't have the responsibility to change him, to make him into the man I want. I leave that up to God. And do you know what happens? God changes *me*. God changes my attitude and works in my life, and then I see my husband changing.

Release Your Husband to Be God's Man

Sometimes we hold our husbands back from being the best they can be. Often this is from our own lack of self-esteem or selfishness. Sometimes it's from guilt.

Let your husband grow. Let him become the man that God has created him to be. Free him and you will be free. We women have great influence over our husbands, more than we usually realize. I want my influence to be a positive one. Don't hold your husband back because of your fears. Let him go!

Will your love with your husband die or grow? That is not altogether up to you; it takes two to make a good marriage. But there is much you can do to improve your chances. Whether you apply them or not is your choice.

A wise old man once lived in a small mountain village. He was greatly respected by the people in that village, and people often went to him to ask advice.

One young man wanted to be wiser than the old man, so he went away to school and then to graduate school. At last he came home, thinking he was wise enough to outwit the old wise man. Taking a live bird in his hand, he went to the old man's home to ask whether the bird was dead or alive. If the old man said dead, he would let the bird go. If he said alive, the young man would squeeze and kill the bird.

When he stood before the old man, he said, "Can you answer this question? I have a bird in my hand. Is he dead or alive?"

The old wise man looked at the young man and quietly replied, "The choice is in your hands."

Love is a choice, and the choice to love your man is in your hands.

Thinking About Love

1. Why does a good marriage take work?

2. What does the Bible mean when it talks about honoring Christ by submitting to each other in Ephesians 5:21?

3. Do this self-examination on the ten things that a man needs from his wife. If you are a married man, indicate how important each of these is to you. If you are a married woman, take the test based on how well you think you do these things for your husband. Score

yourself 1–10, with 1 as the lowest and 10 as the highest:

_____ share your husband's life
_____ build up your husband
_____ value his ideas
_____ honor him in front of the children
_____ be loyal to him
_____ be responsive to his sexual needs
_____ be a team
_____ practice forgiveness
_____ pray for your husband
_____ release your husband to be God's man

12
Love Life and It Will Love You Back

Why do some people seem to have so much more energy than others? A doctor was recently asked this question. His answer was, "It's largely a matter of glands. Some people have energetic glands." He went on to explain that the endocrine glands are mostly responsible for rushing adrenaline into the blood.

Then he was asked, "What activates the glands to secrete the adrenaline?"

The doctor answered, "A positive approach to life."

Do you want more energy? Do you want life to be fun? Do you want to live with enthusiasm? Then this is what you need to do:

> Love life and it will love you back.

The moment you fall in love with a great idea or a cause that is greater than you are, or the moment you begin to love other people, you become creative. Your energy begins to flow; you become charged with enthusiasm; life takes on new meaning. It's fun to be alive when you love life. In this age of cynicism, we need to hear this spiritual truth: Love life and it will love you back.

You see, life is like a boomerang: what you put into it is what comes back to you. The Bible says it this way: "Give, and it will be given to you. A good measure, pressed down, shaken together and running over, will be poured into your lap" (Luke 6:38).

Love Looks for the Best and Finds It

According to *The Living Bible*, love is always positive. Love always looks for the best. "If you love someone you will be loyal to him no matter what the cost. You will always believe in him, always expect the best of him, and always stand your ground in defending him" (1 Corinthians 13:7).

Nothing destroys love like being negative, and without love, you cannot enjoy other people or your surroundings. Negative people never enjoy life. No matter how good they have it, they always find something wrong. A negative man can be married to a beautiful woman with a gentle, loving spirit, and he will find something wrong with her. A negative person can go to the best church in town for a long time and keep seeing things he thinks are wrong. A negative person can have the best job and only talk about what's wrong with it. Centering on the negative wipes out one's love for life.

Warning: Negative people will try to pull you down into the quicksand of despair and despondency. Don't allow them to do it! Run away from negative people, because they are destructive to your health and well-being. In Romans 12:2 (PHILLIPS) we are warned, "Don't let the world around you squeeze you into its own mould." There is so much in life to enjoy, yet many enjoy it very little because they are so negative. Don't let negative people squeeze out your joy and love of life.

The Scripture also tells us, in Romans 12:2, ". . . Be transformed by the renewing of your mind." We have to keep coming to the Lord and getting our minds renewed. The right perspective is to love life and it will love you back.

Do you know there is a right way and a wrong way to pray? I've heard people pray so negatively that I wanted to run. Negative prayers are not pleasing to the Lord. We are to begin our prayers with praises to God; we are to end them with victory. In between, you may share your deepest pain and hurt. Along the way in your prayer you confess your sins, ask for forgiveness, and ask to be cleansed. But the way to pray is to begin with praise and end with victory. Then your mind is renewed and you can get up and go out and love life so it will love you back.

Give Everyone the V.I.P. Treatment

> **Loving life means treating other people as you want to be treated.**

In the Sermon on the Mount, Jesus taught us this very important principle for getting the most out of life and relationships with others: "Treat others as you want them to treat you" (Luke 6:31 TLB).

How do you want to be treated? I want to be treated with respect. I want to be valued as a person of worth. I want to be listened to. I want to be understood. Isn't this what everyone wants? This is the way to get along with other people: Give them what they want.

Have you ever noticed that people treat you differently according to how you are dressed? If you are dressed well and look nice, people treat you one way. Have your old clothes on, and they treat you another way. How do you treat people who are serving you? How about the clerk at the store? How do you act when things go wrong with something you buy? How do you treat the person you take it back to? I had an experience like that recently. Just as I was ready to shoot off my mouth in an unappealing way, Jesus' words came to me: "Whatever you did for one of the least of these brothers of mine, you did for me" (Matthew 25:40). I said, "Oh, oh," and then I treated the clerk with the kindness and understanding I wanted.

People who love life are people who value other people. One thing I noticed about Dr. Norman Vincent Peale when he was in Portland in 1987 for our Church of the Year Award presentation from Guideposts was that he treated every person with respect and valued them. I'll never forget the conversation he had in my office with the mayor of our city. Dr. Peale treated the mayor as if he were the most important person in all the world. He didn't talk about his political position, he simply communicated with him as a person of worth. A little later I noticed that Dr. Peale treated a lady from a very small newspaper as if she were a reporter from *Time* magazine. Here is a man who values people as persons of worth. He loves people, and they love him back.

> **Making other people feel good about themselves is like putting money in the bank. It pays rich dividends.**

As you learn to understand other people so that you can build them up as persons, you are going to create a happier environment for everyone. People are so much easier to live with, work with, and get along with when they have good feelings about themselves. So as you build the self-esteem level of the people you relate to, you are actually making it easier for you to get along with them. You're on the beam when you build someone's self-esteem.

I teach our staff pastors and lay pastors that when

people act weird and seem difficult to get along with, you've got to take the time to find out where they're coming from and what is going on in their lives. You can't treat other people the way they want to be treated until you know what they need.

In working with church boards, I have learned the valuable lesson that it pays to take the time before conducting business to find out where people are and what is going on in their lives. On our church board we have found that a period of time spent in sharing with one another and praying for one another creates a loving, understanding atmosphere in which to conduct the business of the church. As a young pastor many years ago, I learned the hard way that when people have unsolved problems or conflict or misunderstandings in their personal lives, it affects their decision-making processes as members of a board.

To get along well with people, you will need to become an alert student, studying their feelings and needs. Realize that everyone has the same basic needs you have. Here are some of them:

1. Love given and received.
2. Food, shelter, and preservation of life.
3. A feeling of importance.
4. A sense of being needed and useful.
5. Money and the things money will buy.
6. Life after death.
7. Health and happiness.
8. The well-being of children and family members.
9. A craving for fellowship and oneness with God.

But what is the deepest need of every human being? Sigmund Freud, father of psychology, taught that everything you and I do springs from two natures: the sex urge and the desire to be great. John Dewey, leader in the philosophy of American education, said, "The deepest urge in human nature is the desire to be important." Dr. Robert Schuller of the national Christian television program "Hour of Power" says, "The will to self-love is the deepest of all desires." When you sum up, what these leaders in psychology, philosophy of education, and religion are saying is that the greatest need we have as human beings is expressed in this principle: Everyone needs to feel like a somebody.

> **Whenever you help a person feel like a somebody, he will like you for it!**

I believe that even the most struggling person's life could be changed for the better if someone would reach out and make him feel like a somebody. One of the ways you and I can serve our Heavenly Father is to help His other children discover their true worth.

Some years ago, a boy of ten worked in a factory in Naples. He had a burning desire to be a great singer, but his first teacher wiped him out by saying, "You can't sing." To add insult to injury, the teacher said, "You have no voice at all. It sounds like the wind in the shutters."

Fortunately, this boy's mother, who was but a poor

peasant, had the good sense to believe in her son and his capabilities to fulfill the desire of his heart. She put her arms around him, nursed his wounds, and encouraged him not to give up. She praised him by telling him that she loved to hear him sing and that as he worked hard at it he would improve and become a great singer. This mother backed up her belief in her son by going barefoot herself in order to save money to pay for his music lessons.

That mother's belief in her son and her praise gave the boy the courage to pursue his dream. His name? Enrico Caruso, one of the greatest operatic tenors of all time.

Build another person up by believing in him, and you will become a partner in his achievements. Almost everyone responds warmly to the person who reaches out to give him or her a boost. Encourage others to be everything they can be. They will love you for it, and your relationships will be enriched with growing friendship.

What You Give Is What You Get

We need to heed the words Jesus gave us in the Sermon on the Mount: "Try to show as much compassion as your Father does. Never criticize or condemn—or it will all come back on you. Go easy on others; then they will do the same for you. For if you give, you will get! Your gift will return to you in full and overflowing measure, pressed down, shaken together to make room for more, and running over. Whatever measure you use to give—large or small—will be used to measure what is given back to you" (Luke 6:36–38 TLB).

What is Jesus saying here? He is saying that what you give is what you get back. When I was a boy growing up, I had a boomerang. I used to stand and throw it out as far as I could, and it would always circle around and come back to me. Life is like a boomerang: What you give is what you get. If you judge others harshly, you get harsh judging. If you are critical toward others, you get criticism back.

On the other hand, if you send out love messages, love comes back. If you give other people acceptance, acceptance comes back to you. You give other people forgiveness and they give forgiveness. As the Bible says, "A man reaps what he sows" (Galatians 6:7).

Robert Schuller told this story in one of his sermons:

> Once there was a little boy who was strongly admonished and rebuked by his mother. Angry with his mother, he ran out of the house and into the woods. There he stood on the hill and yelled into the forest, "I hate you! I hate you! I hate you!"
>
> Then he heard a voice (his echo) coming back at him, a stranger out of the woods saying, "I hate you! I hate you! I hate you!"
>
> That scared him. He ran back to his mother and said, "Mother, there is a mean man in the woods. He's out there calling and saying, 'I hate you! I hate you! I hate you!' "
>
> His mother, who was very wise, caught on to what was going on and said, "Just a minute, son." She took

him by the hand and led him back out into the woods, up on the hill, and then she said, "Shout as loud as you can into the woods, 'I love you! I love you! I love you!' "

So he did what his mother suggested. He stood there and shouted at the top of his lungs, "I love you! I love you! I love you!"

"So," the mother said, "it is in life. What you send out in life is what comes back to you. Life is like an echo."

Love life and it will love you back!

What Do You Do When Someone Attacks You?

In the Sermon on the Mount, Jesus said, "Love your *enemies*. Do *good* to those who *hate* you. Pray for the happiness of those who *curse* you; implore God's blessing on those who *hurt* you. If someone slaps you on one cheek, let him slap the other too! If someone demands your coat, give him your shirt besides" (Luke 6:27–29 TLB).

What did Jesus mean by this? He was saying never, ever surrender to the negative. When someone does you wrong, don't do something worse in return. If you do, you just compound the trouble. Instead, live by a higher authority, the living words of Jesus. Go on the offensive—*take positive action*.

Be a responder, not a negative reactor.

Is it easy to love? If someone mistreats you, it certainly isn't. In Luke 6:32–35, Jesus explains that anyone can love someone who treats him nicely, but to love someone who is attacking you and being evil toward you takes God's kind of love. To have God's kind of love, we've got to be tuned in to God through knowing Jesus Christ and living in obedience to Him.

When it comes to getting along with people, particularly difficult people, Jesus is our guide and example. Considering all the difficult people Jesus had to deal with, it's a wonder He kept His sanity. They made Him out to be a troublemaker when He was a peacemaker. The Man of love was constantly the object of the hatred of difficult people. Jesus felt their ingratitude, misunderstandings, rejection, and betrayal. When you study Jesus' life and see all the abusive treatment He suffered to serve people, you marvel that He didn't become disturbed Himself.

Yet not once did He allow the bizarre behavior of others to dictate what He would do. Neither did He allow all the misbehavior directed at Him to change His spirit from one of love. Jesus did not allow anyone to sidetrack Him from the will of the Father. With enormous strength and self-control, He lived out the life of loving even His enemies.

In the Bible we read these words: "In this world you will have trouble. But take heart! I have overcome the world" (John 16:33). When we feel overrun and under attack from the misbehavior of difficult people in our lives, we need to move closer to Jesus and draw our strength and direction from Him. Remember, "The one who is in you is greater than the one who is in the world" (1 John 4:4).

Here are some things to remember when you are under attack:

- Remember who you are—a child of God.
- Don't allow yourself to overheat and overreact.
- Refuse to play the difficult person's game.
- Have realistic expectations. Don't keep expecting him or her to play fair.
- Recognize that you can't change the other person's behavior. Give him and the behavior to the Lord.
- Keep your own spirit right with the Lord.
- Refuse to become negative, and keep praying for the person who is hurting you.
- Take positive action.

No matter where you are in your life right now, you can open up to God's love and accept it. With His power within you, start putting love into action and you, too, can overcome evil by doing good.

No matter what has gone wrong in your life, what you need to do is get up and take positive action.

LOVE
   LIFE
      AND
         IT WILL
            LOVE YOU BACK.

Thinking About Love

1. What effect, if any, does a positive or negative approach to life have on your energy level, and why? De-

scribe a person you know who loves life and shows that life loves him or her back.

2. Read 1 Corinthians 13:7 TLB. If you put this kind of love into practice, what kind of attitude will you have?

3. What does Romans 12:2 have to teach us about living with and relating to negative people? How can we keep from being dragged down to their level of existence?

4. List some ways you desire to be treated by others. How do you think others want to be treated by you? List people you are not treating like people of value and ask God to show you how you can improve.

5. Read Luke 6:37–39 and pick out the primary principle that we need to learn and apply in our lives. How is life like a boomerang? (*See* Galatians 6:7.) Give some illustrations.

6. How did Jesus say we are to react to negative treatment? (Read Luke 6:27–36.) Make a list of the positive actions you can take to counter negative actions against you.

13
Love Will Win the World

What is the value of one human soul?

When you die, what do you leave behind? What do you take with you? In this chapter we will answer these penetrating questions.

Stories about children have a way of staying in my heart when I have long forgotten other stories. The following story about little Johnnie is one of my favorites. Maybe it's because the story is set in Chicago, and I went to college just south of Chicago, at Olivet Nazarene College, in Kankakee, Illinois. In the winter, I thought Kankakee was the coldest place on earth!

As the story goes, it was a cold Sunday in Chicago and Dwight L. Moody's Sunday school was operating as it did every Sunday. Arriving late in the morning was a little boy whose legs were blue from the severe cold wind blowing across Lake Michigan.

His coat was tattered and torn and pulled together at

the top with a safety pin. Johnnie had no hat on his head to keep him warm. His worn-out shoes had holes in the bottom, and he wore no socks.

Taking the boy in her arms, the Sunday-school greeter began to massage his half-frozen legs to stimulate the circulation. Then, setting the boy down at arm's length, she asked him where he lived. When Johnnie told her, the Sunday-school greeter realized he had walked more than two miles across the windy city of Chicago, on a bleak January morning, to attend the Sunday school of Dwight L. Moody.

"Why did you do it?" asked the friendly greeter. "You must have walked past a dozen churches to come here. Why?" The little boy was shy, and he hesitated a moment before he blurted out, "I guess, ma'am, it was because here they love a fellow."

Believe me—love will win the world!

A war is waged for the destiny of every person. Unlike other weapons that break, divide, and destroy, God's weapon of love heals, fulfills, and brings man back to Him again.

This promise is yours: "In all these things we are more than conquerors through him who loved us" (Romans 8:37).

The Value of a Human Soul

You were given your worth at birth. In Genesis 1:27 we read, "So God created man in his own image, in the image of God he created him; male and female he created them."

Man was first created a physical being. God created him physically before He breathed into him the breath of life (*see* Genesis 2:7). After his sin, man was told by God, "Dust you are and to dust you will return " (Genesis 3:19). Therefore, man has a temporary body that dies and decays. Isn't it interesting that that part of the person which is only temporary receives so much attention in modern life? Look at the billions of dollars we spend on cosmetics, perfumes, deodorants, hairstyles, diets, and exercise.

> **Yet the physical body as we know it is only the temporary dwelling!**

In the New Testament, Jesus makes a clear distinction between the soul and the body: "Do not be afraid of those who kill the body but cannot kill the soul. Rather, be afraid of the One who can destroy both soul and body in hell" (Matthew 10:28).

What is the soul? The soul controls our will and desires and has power over the physical body. Your soul contains your mind and all your thought processes. The soul also comprises that which we call emotions: love, joy, and fear.

Where did the soul come from? Your soul did not just evolve from a worm or a monkey or some lower existence. It was created by Almighty God Himself. In Genesis 2:7 we read, "The Lord God formed the man from the dust of the ground and breathed into his nostrils the breath of life, and the man became a living being."

What is man? This is a very important question, one that David asked in Psalms 8. David was a shepherd before he was a king, so he spent many a night out looking at the stars. One of those clear nights when he was looking up at the stars, overwhelmed by the magnitude of God's creation, he asked this question: "What is man that you are mindful of him, the son of man that you care for him?" (Psalms 8:4).

What was David feeling and experiencing? Man is insignificant if you consider only his physical size. In comparison with the vastness of the earth, he is only a speck. When you become aware of the solar system in which our earth is located, man becomes even less significant. Then, when you realize that one visible star is millions of times larger than our own solar system, man becomes, by comparison, totally insignificant. David's question is a penetrating one. "What is man that you are mindful of him?"

What gives man dignity is the fact that the Creator of our vast universe has chosen to center attention on him, not only by creating him but by sending His Son Jesus to save him.

Man is not only dignified by God's creation, attention, and sacrificing of His own Son, but he is dignified by his high calling. What is our calling on this earth? Psalms 8:5, 6 tells us, "You made him a little lower than the heavenly beings and crowned him with glory and honor. You made him ruler over the works of your hands; you put everything under his feet." Of all God's creation, you are His choice. He has given you dominion over all the rest of His creation. How much is your soul worth? It is worth more than all of God's creation.

Jesus came to tell and show us how much a soul is worth. In comparing the worth of your soul with all the other things on this earth, He said, "What good is it for a man to gain the whole world, yet forfeit his soul? Or what can a man give in exchange for his soul?" (Mark 8:36, 37). The bottom line is: *nothing* is worth more than your soul!

The soul is eternal. I knew an older man who denied the reality of death by saying, "*If* I die." When it comes to the reality of death, there are no ifs; it is *when* I die. The Bible says, "What is your life? You are a mist that appears for a little while and then vanishes" (James 4:14).

But the soul never dies. Your soul was created to live forever and ever. Your soul will spend all eternity somewhere. How do you make sure your soul is going to heaven? It seems to me that this is the primary question of life—one we must answer rightly. Compared to this, all else is insignificant.

How Do You Save Your Soul?

Do you know what is the number-one cause of death in the world? It is not airplane crashes, automobile wrecks, cancer, or AIDS. The number-one cause of death is heart problems. Before you are issued a policy, insurance companies want to know if you have had any heart problems, and they want to know if your relatives had any. Heart problems are very serious.

Scores of people also suffer from emotional heartache. Is anything more painful than to have your heart broken and your dreams dashed into a million pieces?

Yet there is a heart problem more serious than a physical ailment, dangerous as that is. There is a heart problem more serious than having your heart broken emotionally, painful as that can be. There is a heart problem that, if it is not taken care of, will cause you to lose your soul.

When the Bible refers to the heart, it is referring to the center or core of our soul—the center where we make decisions; the center of our affections. For example, in Proverbs 23:7 (KJV), it says, "For as he thinketh in his heart, so is he."

In Jeremiah we read these descriptive words about our heart problem: "The heart is deceitful above all things and beyond cure. Who can understand it? I the Lord search the heart and examine the mind, to reward a man according to his conduct, according to what his deeds deserve" (Jeremiah 17:9, 10).

What can we do about our heart problem? We cannot correct the problem by ourselves. Education will not do it. Knowledge will not do it. Reforming ourselves will not change the heart.

A man named Nicodemus came to Jesus with a heart problem that was destroying him from within and leading him to eternal destruction. Jesus' answer was that Nicodemus needed to be born again. We, too, must experience a supernatural birth.

When Jesus was in the Garden of Gethsemane just before being accused, falsely convicted, and crucified, He said to His disciples, "My soul is overwhelmed with sorrow to the point of death. Stay here and keep watch with me" (Matthew 26:38). Jesus' soul was taking on the heart disease that is ours. To become our solution, He took on our problem. He took unto His own soul our sin and became accursed in our place.

"With his stripes we are healed" (Isaiah 53:5 KJV). By His death, Jesus atoned for our sin. How do we save our souls? We can't! But Jesus does it for us! And when we receive Jesus as our Savior and Lord, through Him and in Him our souls are saved throughout all eternity. "For God so loved the world that he gave his one and only Son, that whoever believes in him shall not perish but have eternal life" (John 3:16).

How to Help Others

The unsaved person doesn't give two hoots about saving anyone's else's soul. The unsaved person doesn't give two hoots about giving any money or effort to saving souls in his own hometown or any other place in the world. The unsaved person doesn't give two hoots about being involved in ministry for the purpose of saving souls.

Do you know what is one of the first things that happens to a saved person? He wants to save everybody else. It feels so wonderful to be forgiven. He is so joyful to be rid of those sins and to have a new heart. He is thrilled to become a brand-new person in Christ. The saved person wants to save everybody else!

If you have little or no interest in saving souls, you had better get on your knees to check out the condition of your own heart. A saved person wants to see other people saved. A saved person rejoices with the angels in heaven when other people are brought to Jesus. A saved person will do anything he can to bring others to Christ.

How do you save souls? Do you stand on the corner and yell at people, "Repent, or go to hell"? Do you go around seeing everybody you know and, not allowing them to say a word, just tell them how to get saved?

I remember a story about a special boy who was retarded and was shopping with his sister at a busy store during the Christmas season. In all the rush he bumped up against a stack of shoes and knocked them all over. The irate clerk grabbed him by the arm, applying pressure, and told him to get down and pick them up. The boy, in shock and rebellion, stood there and shook his head, saying, "No, no." The clerk began to yell all the more and applied more pressure.

The alert and sensitive sister got down on the floor, held her hand out to her brother, and, helping him down, began to show him how to pick up the shoes. After the shoes were all picked up, they stood. The sister looked the irate clerk right in the eyes and said, "Mister, you gotta love him into doing it."

You have to love people to Christ.

How do you do that? You earn the right to share by the way you care for them. You listen. You have compassion. You're interested in them. And then the Holy Spirit will give you the moment, the opportunity, to tell them about Jesus.

About 90 percent of the people who are Christians today are not Christians because a pastor or evangelist brought them to Christ. Ninety percent of all Christians were brought to Christ by laypeople who met them where they were and loved them into coming to Christ.

There are so many people in your world who need to see Jesus in your life.

The man had overslept and was late for his important flight to Chicago. He was running down the corridor at Portland International Airport, trying desperately to make it to the gate before the plane left. He tripped over a little boy and knocked him down. The little boy lay there on the floor crying. At that moment the man had a choice. Would he leave the little boy lying there crying by himself in order to make his flight? Or would he stop, maybe miss his plane, and help the child? Because he was a sensitive, caring follower of Jesus, he inconvenienced himself in that moment. He knelt down and ministered to the little boy's needs. In that moment came the payoff. The little boy looked up into his eyes and asked, "Mister, are you Jesus?"

For that moment, that day, the man became Jesus to a little boy. Jesus said, "By this all men will know that you are my disciples, if you love one another" (John 13:35).

> **Love is the way you win others to Christ.**

Recently someone shared this line with me: You can give without loving, but you cannot love without giving. Isn't that good? You cannot love without giving. How do you win others to Christ? By giving of yourself in attention, interest, and love to them. If your mate unsaved, you are not going to win that mate to Christ by withholding your love. You don't win anyone withholding your love. Remember! You have to love them into becoming Christians.

A woman in a large city was attending an evening meeting at her downtown church. Not giving it a second thought, she left her car in a parking lot under care and supervision of the attendant, with the key it at his request. A couple of hours later, when returned to pick up her car, it was nowhere to be found. The parking lot attendant didn't have the faintest what had happened to her missing automobile.

What would you say to the parking lot attendant your car were missing? Expecting a wave of accusation

and big trouble from the owner of the missing vehicle, the attendant became very defensive.

What happened next is unbelievable. There is no way to understand it but to realize that Jesus Christ was present in the life of this woman. Presented with a panic-button-pressing situation, she kept her cool. This Christian woman refused to react in a hateful or vindictive manner. With calm assurance, she told the parking lot attendant that it was just an automobile and she believed that God would take care of this problem. How true it is that the greater the crisis, the greater the opportunity to witness to God's love. The man was astounded. Never before had he seen such overcoming love.

The next Sunday who should attend the woman's church? You guessed it—the parking lot attendant and his entire family. Better yet, I am told they have been there every Sunday since, and now they are sitting close to the front!

A couple of weeks later, the lady's expensive car was found parked a few miles away, with no damage whatsoever.

Love will win the world!

Thinking About Love

1. What value did Jesus place on the soul? (*See* Mark 8:35–37.)

2. How do you save your soul? Can we do enough to save ourselves? (Read Ephesians 2:8, 9.)

3. What heart problem is more severe than heart disease or even emotional heartache? (Read Jeremiah 17:9, 10.) What must happen to take care of this heart problem so we can make heaven our home? (*See* John 3.)

4. When you receive Jesus Christ and are saved, what is the first thing that you want to do?

5. How do you save the lost souls in your area and others whose lives you touch? How do you love the people in your world into becoming Christians?